Nance, a woman of creativity
and commitment

Copyright © 1981 by Donald A. Tubesing

No part of this book may be reproduced or transmitted in any for
tronic or mechanical, including photocopying, without permission
ublisher. For information address Whole Person Associates, Inc
P.O. Box 3151. Duluth, Minnesota 55803.

Published by arrangement with the author

ET TRADEMARK REG. U.S. PAT. OFF. AND FOREIGN COUNTRIES
REGISTERED TRADEMARK—MARCA REGISTRADA
HECHO EN CHICAGO, U.S.A.

SIGNET CLASSIC, MENTOR, PLUME, MERIDIAN AND NAL BOOKS
are published by New American Library,
1633 Broadway, New York, New York 10019

First Signet Printing, October, 1982

3 4 5 6 7 8 9 10 11

PRINTED IN THE UNITED STATES OF AMERICA

SIGHTING AND DEFEATING "THE INVISIBLE KILLER"

Cancer . . . heart attacks . . . arthritis . . . ulcers . . . headaches . . . upset stomachs . . . are but a few of the crippling diseases related to stress in America today.

Now this stress can be recognized, dramatically reduced and even turned to your advantage through the stress-control program developed and taught by psychologist Donald A. Tubesing, whose work in this area has won him high professional renown and nationwide success.

This amazingly simple and effective program has been recorded in a wise and helpful book that will teach you all the many ways in which you can counter the harmful effects of stress. It is the finest stress-control self-help guide on the market today. Read it. And relax.

KICKING YOUR STRESS HABITS
A DO-IT-YOURSELF GUIDE FOR COPING WITH STRESS

ABOUT THE AUTHOR:
DONALD A. TUBESING, MDiv, PhD., psychologist, educator, minister and consultant, lives with his family in Duluth, Minnesota, where canoeing and cross-country skiing are among his favorite de-stressors.

KICK
YO
STR
HAB

A DO-IT-YO
GUIDE
COPING WIT

DONALD A. TUB

A SIGNET

NEW AMERICA

CONTENTS

The feeling of thankfulness reduces stress. I am full of gratitude for the many people who have contributed their energy to enhance the quality of this project.

The following deserve public recognition for all their behind-the-scenes efforts.
Nancy Loving Tubesing—a long-suffering accomplice
Laura Loving—a walking thesaurus
Jennifer Bolch—a magician with words
Bruce Carlton—a designer original
Vicki Morrison Goble—the original Flying Fingers
Bill Peterson—and my colleagues at
                        the Wholistic Health Centers
Artie Pine—for encouragement and support

Others who read and commented on the manuscript during its evolution, or who typed and re-typed major portions, include:
Barb Baldwin   Karen Makowski
Ellen Batchelder   Salvinija Kernaghan
Mary Boman   Liz Medes
Karen Contardo   Michael Scherschligt
Katherine Harris   Mary O'Brien Sippel
David Hibbard   Hazel Zimner

1/ STRESS ILLS or STRESS SKILLS

Questions and answers about stress

9505 San Bonita Avenue, Apartment 106, 5:45 pm, Friday

... *"Oh, no, I forgot the casserole!"*

Barbara Fitzgerald dashed for the kitchen, alerted by the smell of burning rice. She grabbed for the hot pan, yelling as she flinched and dropped it. She watched as the pan hit the floor and supper spilled across the tiles.

Then she leaned against the counter and started to cry. Why did she botch everything? Visions of her fights with Tom flooded back. Here, in this very kitchen before their divorce last year. . . . Her stomach felt hollow. All the old hurt and anger and helplessness welled up.

Barbara tried to tell herself what a competent person she was. Good at her job. A loving mother. But deep down inside, she feared that she wasn't. Those feelings of inadequacy just wouldn't go away.

And she felt so alone. Even the party invitation from the Weston's didn't help. She just didn't feel like going anywhere . . . alone . . . again.

Would she ever get over that failed marriage? Barbara noticed the familiar, dull throbbing at the base of her skull, a sensation that signaled another one of her blinding headaches.

9505 San Bonita Avenue, Apartment 107, 5:45 pm, Friday

. . . *Kathy Weston was hurrying, too, mixing the bacon and onions with sour cream, slicing the vegetables. Her guests would arrive in less than two hours. She felt flushed and eager. Kathy loved planning a party, loved the excitement, the attention.*

She looked forward to seeing all the friends she and Larry had made in the six months since their move here, to having them all together for the first time in her home.

Would they all come? Would they mix well? The challenge of the occasion only stimulated her more.

"How lovely she is," Larry mused as he helped Kathy prepare the punch. He was bursting to tell her his great news—the rumor of a promotion and the possibility of a move back to Philadelphia, where they both grew up. But he decided to wait till later to surprise her.

And, pleased as he was, he couldn't help wondering how she would take the news of another move.

9505 San Bonita Avenue, Apartment 108, 5:45 pm, Friday

. . . *"Supper's on," Lola called, and Henry Schmidt heaved himself up from the couch and moved slowly to the table. He poked at his food and tried to make small talk about his day at work. But office politics seemed so unimportant and far away.*

The room was oppressively quiet. As usual, the silence set off that awful feeling of emptiness, reminding Henry—not that he ever really forgot—that his son, Carl, his rambunctious, freckle-faced boy, was gone. Dead. Never to throw a baseball, or slam a door, or give his father that wonderful, crooked smile of his again.

Henry wanted to scream, "It's not fair!" Instead, he launched his nightly litany of petty slights and slip-ups of the day, complaining about all the unfair people he had encountered.

Lola sat as usual, nodding in silence. She had so little energy these days. Better just to let Henry ramble on than to interrupt and become yet another unfair force in his world.

9505 San Bonita Avenue, Apartment 109, 5:45 pm, Friday

. . . *"Dad's home, Daddy's home,"* Pat and Lisa ran up the stairs shouting. *"Now we can pack the car and go!"*

Pete Kowalski was exhausted from late-night packing and a day spent getting the office in order so he could leave for a week's vacation. His fatigue faded as he warmed to his children's contagious enthusiasm. In two hours they'd be at the lake, watching the moon rise over the pines.

Lynn sighed and straightened her damp bandana as she bent over the last stack of towels. The dishes were done, the suitcases packed, the frisbee found, and the groceries bought. It had been a long day. But Lynn felt a growing excitement as she realized that their long-awaited week out of the city was really about to begin.

9505 San Bonita Avenue, Apartment 110, 5:45 pm, Friday

. . . *Abigail Thomas sat watching TV, the blinds half-drawn. She heard the Kowalski children shouting and doors slamming as they carried groceries and camping gear out to the car.*

"I do wish they'd stop making such a racket," she groused to herself. Why did she have to put up with the painful reminder of her own busier days gone by? Sighing, Mrs. Thomas wondered if she should bother fixing some supper for herself or just go to sleep.

The apartment building at 9505 San Bonita Avenue is filled with people—people filled with stress. All homes are. All people are.

Does everyone experience stress?

Yes, stress is part of everyday life. Burning the supper, living with divorce, hosting a party, receiving a promotion, moving, losing a child, going on vacation, living alone . . . stress is a fact of life.

But, contrary to popular belief, stress is not the pressure from the outside—the divorce, the death, the burned supper, the vacation, the isolation. Those are **stressors.** Your response to those situations constitutes **stress.**

The distinction is important. Stressors are the multitude of daily occurrences that call upon you to adapt. Stress is your response as you attempt to make the adjustment.

How many potentially stressful situations have you already adjusted to today?

Is stress good or bad for me?

It can be either. Some stress is good. Stress will help Kathy Weston be a more dynamic hostess. Stress energizes the Kowalski's as they prepare for their trip.

Everyone needs stress sometimes. Gearing up to drive on ice, fighting for your rights, meeting a deadline, preparing for Christmas, making it through a crisis on raw courage, cramming for an exam, making a terrific impression at a job interview, walking into a room full of strangers at a party—all demand the stimulation of positive stress.

Stress can be a turn-on. It can pump you up, give you energy, supply that zest for living.

But stress can also become destructive. It can turn into distress. It can gnaw away at you and sap your energy over the months and years. Barbara Fitzgerald is drained from the stress of her divorce, as are Lola and Henry Schmidt from the death of their son. Distress can also come from less traumatic events, such as fighting with someone you love, expecting too much of yourself, turning every little setback into a crisis, or sacrificing sleep to add a few minutes to your work day.

Distress, whether it comes from major or relatively minor traumas, can wear you out.

Stress is like spice—in the right proportion it enhances the flavor of a dish. Too little produces a bland, dull meal; too much may choke you. Like the violin string that needs enough tension to make music but not so much that it snaps, you have an appropriate level of stress. The trick is to find it.

How can I tell when stress becomes distress?

Your body will tell you about your stress. With a tight throat, sweaty palms, an aching head, fatigue, nausea, diarrhea, a vague uneasiness—it will send you signals when you're suffering distress.

Frequent headaches may be a sign that you're mentally overloaded and, like Barbara Fitzgerald, you're hanging on to your head for fear of losing control.

Your aching shoulders might be saying, "You're carrying too much of a burden . . . relax . . . let down . . . loosen up."

Your aching back may be begging, "Stand up for yourself."

Your indigestion may be reminding you of everything you've had to "stomach" recently.

If you discover that you're more tired, depressed, frustrated or restless than usual; if your relationships are no longer satisfying; if your sleeping patterns change or your weight goes up or down dramatically, you may be experiencing too much or too little stress. Generally, you'll know which one.

Your body, mind and spirit will send you their distress signals. Be aware. Listen to yourself.

What can I do about my stress?

Once your personal distress signals let you know that the stress in your life needs attention, the management decisions are up to you. Stress management doesn't mean getting rid of all stress. Rather, it means making thoughtful choices about which stress to keep and which to let go.

Like Barbara Fitzgerald or the Schmidts, you may be suffering from stress overload. If so, coping will probably involve a decision to "turn down the juice," at least a bit.

Or you may be suffering from stress underload, like Abigail Thomas. If so, you will probably need to "turn up the juice" by finding additional stimulation and challenge.

What if I ignore my stress?

Ignore your stress and it gets worse. It can also make you sick. The latest medical literature suggests that either stress overload or underload may be hazardous to your health. In fact, some authorities believe that up to 90 percent of all illness is stress-related.

With all the demands of modern life—the changing roles of men and women, inflation, recession, the pressure to succeed—many people fall victim to the high stress diseases of adaptation: peptic ulcers, chronic headaches, heart disease, high blood pressure and anxiety.

With the loneliness of the elderly, the isolation of suburbia, the loss of meaning in many jobs, the lack of physical challenge and addiction to TV, almost as many people suffer from low stress disorders, the diseases of stagnation: depression, digestive disturbances, spirit-crushing boredom.

You probably don't really want to make yourself sick from stress overload or underload. But you may be doing it by the choices you make. Choices about the work you do, where you live, whom you love, how you play, what you consider important.

How can stress skills help me?

Everyone at 9505 San Bonita is experiencing stress. For some, it's stress they want to savor. Kathy Weston is turned on by her party preparations. Larry is charged up about his impending promotion and his desire to return to Philadelphia. The Kowalski's are bursting with excitement about their upcoming vacation.

Stress is adding spice to Kathy and Larry and Pete and Lynn and Pat and Lisa's lives. So they'll probably want to keep it. They could use this book to affirm and strengthen the positive power of stress in their lives.

Not everyone would experience these pressures as positive, of course. One person's pleasure is another's poison. Some would lose sleep or worry themselves sick if they were faced with a party, a promotion or a trip. For such people, the very stress that energizes Kathy or Larry or Lynn could cause them trouble. They could use this book to identify what is distressing them and find new ways of coping with their stress.

With major stress

Some of the residents of 9505 San Bonita are experiencing severe stress. For Henry and Lola Schmidt, the loss of little Carl has left a hole that can never be filled. The sense of not being wanted is turning Abigail Thomas' apartment into a prison. As Barbara Fitzgerald tried to keep her head above water emotionally, stress stalks her.

There are no simple solutions to the stress of divorce, of the death of a child, of being alone, of any of life's great sorrows. Things will never be the same again for Barbara or Henry or Lola or Abigail.

This book won't help them bring back the past. But it can help them find new ways to take control of their lives again, to hope again and to take better care of themselves.

They may also need to reach out to friends or to seek the help of a professional as they struggle to grow through their pain.

Almost everyone has experienced some major personal disaster. We're all scarred veterans of one battle or another. If you're living with high intensity stress right now, this book can offer you lots of suggestions or places to start. It can't make major, or even minor, wounds go away, but it can help you develop a more positive self-image and identify coping techniques that will work for YOU.

With minor stress

Most stress is not caused by the great tragedies of life, however. Most of it comes from the accumulation of minor irritants that steadily grind us down over the years.

You determine the amount of wear and tear these day-to-day pressures cause by your viewpoint, by the attitudes you hold and by the choices you make. If you're experiencing this kind of garden-variety stress, this book can help you discover both how you are creating your own stress and how you can get rid of it. It will help you recognize personal strengths you may have neglected and learn to make the life choices only you can make.

Sometimes you may need support from family and friends or even professional help. At other times, you just need to be self-aware and self-reflective.

What's the first step?

What you have in your hands is far more than a book—it's an experience. To get the most out of the experience, don't just read it. DO IT.

In Chapters 2 and 3 you will discover how your viewpoint and your beliefs are the underlying cause of stress. You can compare your experience with the special cases of stressors (change, life stages, loss and rhythm) outlined in Chapters 4-7. Identify your alternatives for coping in the stress skills section (Chapters 8-13). Finally, be sure to use the planning guide at the end of the book to design specific strategies for coping with the most troublesome of your current stressors.

Each chapter is full of questions for you to think about and answer. Read this book with pencil in hand and make it yours by recording your observations and insights.

2/ PERCEPTION and STRESS

How you stress yourself

The wedding's over!

Dearest Nana,

Everything went so well! (Except for the flowers, but I'm sure I was the only one who noticed.) The ushers, God love 'em, took my meddling patiently. You know how I can be—and this wedding was so important to me.

It was certainly no Emily Post special, but people enjoyed themselves so much, it didn't matter. Everyone seemed to understand when we had to use those old napkins advertising the bank (remember those?). In fact, they were good for a few wisecracks and a lot of laughter.

Oh, and they really enjoy being together. I'm so pleased that my daughter is marrying into such a caring family.

They were such good sports! I'm sure they felt awkward handling those delicate champagne glasses, but they just chuckled. And by the time I'd had a few(!) sips of their beer, I was chuckling, too.

Would you believe that I got out on the dance floor trying to polka? Folks just seemed to clear a path for me and smiled when they saw me coming.

I'm sure that most of our friends had never attended a wedding reception like that! And to think I was the hostess for such an interesting mix of people.

So now Charlotte is off to play mother to 250 piglets (is that what you call them?). She'll probably get big muscles and a red neck from working out on the farm. But I don't think her smile will fade soon, and that's what I care about.

9

I feel good all over. What a day to remember! Just wanted to share the good news with you.

Always,

Ginger

Dearest Nana,

I made it! . . . barely. I've already had one good cry (by myself, of course), but I wanted to get this off to you. You wouldn't believe all the things that went wrong.

The florist sent an impossible arrangement. Luckily, I had time to redo all the flowers myself . . . in between my run-ins with the ushers. They knew NOTHING about wedding etiquette, so I really lit into them a couple of times. What else could I do?

I have such a headache! But nothing now, compared to the moment when I realized that the monogrammed napkins weren't going to arrive.

To top it all off, of course, I can hardly stand my new son-in-law. I just don't know how my daughter could marry a man like him. He's always guffawing over some joke—that I find embarrassing.

And his family! All those uncles bumping into one another's beer bellies and hugging! I was sure I'd turn around and find them eating the peas with their knives. It's a good thing we had beer—they hung around the keg all evening. I thought they were going to crush those beautiful champagne glasses with their bare hands!

You wouldn't have believed the band they dug up. When it started playing those awful, loud polkas . . .

I couldn't even look at our other friends. I'm sure they've never been to a wedding like this. Have you ever heard of such a disaster?

Well, I did it the way Charlotte wanted. I hope she's happy. I can't imagine how she could be, though, marrying into a family of farmers and moving to a pig farm!

At least I don't have to go through this again.

Thanks for listening,
Always,

Rosemary

Two mothers' viewpoints

It's the same wedding . . . or is it? The events are the same, but notice how different the experiences are.

Both weddings are stress-full. Most weddings are. But Ginger feels exhilarated, Rosemary, exhausted. The difference clearly is in their viewpoints.

The events themselves—ushers showing people to the wrong seats, phantom napkins, wedding guests dancing polkas—are neutral, neither good nor bad, stressful nor unstressful. They get their positive or negative charge from the meanings Ginger and Rosemary assign to them.

Rosemary perceives the unexpected as threatening. Not surprisingly, she worries and fusses, feeling distressed by all the hitches that spoiled the day for her. Ginger finds those same surprises stimulating and she's not afraid to laugh at herself. As a result, she enjoys the wedding.

Stress is in your point of view

Like these mothers of the bride, you determine the stress you experience. It's really a matter of viewpoint. Some events will be more stressful for you than others—the degree of stress depends on your interpretation of them. So your stress is all in your mind! This doesn't imply that your stress (or Rosemary's) is phony. Not at all. It does suggest that your perceptions, the meanings you assign to events, are at the root of your stress.

What an exciting door that opens! If you create your stress by your mental attitude, you can get rid of it by changing your mind. More about that later.

First, let's look at how you create stress by your perceptions.

Let's say you wake up at 7:28 a.m.

Is that early or late? Is your first glance at the clock alarming or comforting?

If you were due at an 8:00 meeting and your office is half an hour from home; if you were supposed to have your children at the bus stop by 7:15; if your boss was expecting a call from you at 7:00, you're likely to experience a familiar, sinking feeling, muttering, "Oh, no, late again!" as you leap out of bed in a frenzy, setting off a chain reaction of minor disasters that reinforces your growing fear that this is going to be "one of those days."

On the other hand, if it's your day off, or if your alarm was set for 8:15, you might just stretch luxuriously, roll over and snuggle down for another 40 winks.

In both cases, the event was the same. The clock read 7:28. But your reactions were very different. Each depended on the meaning you assigned to its being 7:28.

Where do perceptions come from?

We learn to interpret our experiences very early in life. We learn from our parents, our teachers, our peers. Kids are natural mimics. They imitate and assimilate the behavior they see.

Sandy hears ongoing arguments about money; sees Dad getting short-tempered and jittery at income tax time, guzzling cup after cup of coffee and snapping at anyone who interrupts him; witnesses Mother's hedging with bill collectors on the phone. As an adult, Sandy will probably react with stress to situations involving finances.

Thirteen-year-old Karen wants to understand her developing sexuality. Her mother says, "Ask your teacher." Her teacher says, "Ask your minister." Her minister says, "Ask your mother." From this conspiracy of silence Karen learns to assign a meaning to sex and sexuality: "It's something too awful to discuss."

At her daughter's wedding to the pig farmer, Ginger, who heard a lot of happy laughter in her home as she was growing up, sees the boisterous high spirits of her son-in-law's family as signs of warmth and caring. Rosemary, whose youthful highjinks were almost always squelched with the stern admonition, "Children should be seen and not heard," cringes at the "childish" antics of her daughter's in-laws.

Parents and teachers aren't the only ones who train your perceptions. You learn to assign meanings from the very culture you live in—your ethnic group, your neighborhood, your colleagues, your

church, your geographic location, your friends. Television, books, movies, billboards, newspapers and magazines all powerfully influence the way you view the world.

What difference does it make?

Over the years you absorb the perceptions of those around you, barely even noticing the lessons you've learned. Then something happens and you "know" what it means. Someone smiles at you and you "know" that he's heard a rumor about you, that she's caught you napping, that he's on the make. Every day you encounter a thousand events which you interpret as threatening or non-threatening based on the perception habits you've developed over your lifetime.

Any event can be viewed as potentially harmful. If the meaning you assign to an incident is threatening, you trigger your stress reaction. You will feel most threatened, and so will experience the most stress, when something endangers the people/places/possessions you consider most valuable to you, such as your marriage, your children, your job, your home or your status in the community.

How about you? Grab a pencil and look at the link between stress and perception in your life.

STOP AND REFLECT

- What are some of the stressors in your life that are giving you the most trouble right now?
- What meanings do you assign to each of these stressors?
- When you say something is stressful, you're automatically saying that something important to you is threatened. What of value in your life is threatened by each of the stressors you list?

(Continued)

STRESSOR

too much work to do

_____

_____

MEANING

"can't go away Saturday"

"I'm failing at my job"

_____

_____

_____

_____

THREAT

no time for play

job security, self-esteem

_____

_____

_____

_____

Taking a second look

Just as you assign meanings to situations by habit, so you suffer habitual stress.

You don't usually stop to analyze what meaning you should assign to an experience. Your "decision" is an automatic process and may produce stress before you know what has happened. However, even after you've stressed yourself by interpreting an event as threatening, you can still reduce the amount of stress you're experiencing by taking a second look, by "relabeling".

Rosemary could significantly reduce her distress by relabeling, choosing to interpret the events of her daughter's wedding more like Ginger did. The embarrassment of using old napkins advertising the bank would be transformed into "good-humored banter". The awkwardness of uncle-hugging could become evidence of the warm, caring family her daughter is marrying into. Rowdy polka music would offer an invitation to frolic.

Relabeling is simple, very simple, but it isn't easy. It's tough to break old habits. Relabeling is the first step in kicking your perception habits.

How can I modify my perception habits?

First, when you start to feel stress, retrace your steps until you find the event you have perceived as threatening. Second, identify what meaning you attached to the experience. Finally, if you don't like the way you feel, you can consciously change your mind and choose a different, more positive interpretation.

Now, picture yourself on a downtown street, feeling uptight and depressed. Your hands are clenched and sweaty. Your breath is shallow and your face feels flushed.

Thinking back, you realize that those stress signals were activated after you walked past two of your friends conversing on the corner. When you said, "Hello," neither one responded.

You said to yourself, "Maybe they don't like me anymore," and now you feel uneasy, hurt and resentful.

You don't have to hang on to those feelings. You can short-circuit your perception habits by relabeling what happened.

You could say to yourself:

- "Perhaps neither of them heard me."
- "Phew! I'm glad I wasn't drawn into a long conversation with them in this heat."

- "Maybe they're involved in some conflict. I'll try to show them special kindness the next time I see them."
- "I wonder if they're planning a surprise party for me?"

Any one of these alternative interpretations of the situation could alleviate your distress.

STOP AND REFLECT

- Name a stressful event.
- What was so awful about it?
- How else could you interpret the same event?

STRESSFUL EVENT

missed my bus

_____

_____

_____

THREAT MEANING

"I'll be late"

_____

_____

_____

POSITIVE MEANING

"Now I can read the paper"

_____

_____

_____

Every day will give you hundreds of opportunities to choose labels for what happens to you. You forget the punch line of a joke, you hear angry voices, you wake up with a cold, your friends drink all your Diet Rite, you see dark clouds on the horizon. Are these events stressful? It's up to you. Choose the meaning you want to give them.

Is relabeling always appropriate?

You can't, and shouldn't, relabel all stressful situations. Some situations are truly threatening and deserve high energy stress responses.

If you're taking a walk and a dog jumps out of the bushes with teeth bared, you'd be foolish to try to relabel it as "a romp with Rin Tin Tin". If your friend suddenly becomes very ill, it would be unwise for either of you to relabel it as "a wonderful chance to learn from the pain of life", at least until a doctor has been consulted.

When the threat you perceive in a situation is quite real, go ahead and gear up to fight. You can harness the energy generated by your physical stress reaction and apply it to the problem at hand. You can sprint away from the German shepherd. You can rush your friend to the Emergency Room.

Balancing your stress budget

But don't waste your stress energy. Most people stress themselves unnecessarily in situations that aren't really dangerous. Before gearing up to fight, ask yourself:

* Does a threat really exist?
* Is the issue really important to me?
* Can I make a difference?

If the answer to any of these questions is "no", don't waste your energy. . . . It's not worth it.

It is possible to spend $10 worth of energy on a 10¢ problem.

Are you overspending?

Have you ever fought stubbornly for your point of view when you knew that what you said wouldn't make any difference, that no one cared and even if they had, the point wasn't worth all the trouble? Have you ever kept trying to please someone when it was obvious that nothing could really satisfy him or her? Have you ever felt furious when someone cut into line ahead of you?

If so, you know what it's like to overspend your stress energy.

STOP AND REFLECT

- What are two recent situations in which you spent $10 worth of adrenalin on a 10¢ problem?

  raging about the bikes in the driveway, panicking over "misplaced" keys

  _____

  _____

  _____

  _____

Are you underspending?

On the other hand, it's possible to underspend.

Have you ever allowed a relationship to disintegrate, admitting only after it ended how important it was to you? Have you ever ignored signs of trouble with your children until the problems were nearly too big to handle? Have you ever closed your eyes to injustice on your doorstep, in your own church, club or community, because it was easier not to speak up?

If so, you know what it means to spend 10¢ worth of adrenalin on a $10 problem.

STOP AND REFLECT

- Name two recent situations when you felt underspent, giving insufficient attention to a big problem.

  not defending Bill with his teacher, pigeon-holing
  the overdue tax bill

Underspending is as wasteful as overspending. Wise budgeting of stress energy, like wise budgeting of money, calls for some value judgments. Spend your stress energy by all means—it's a powerful resource—but spend it on the situations in your life that are really important to you.

How can you tell what's most important to you? The next chapter will help you to discover the internal belief system that shapes your perceptions, motivates your actions and determines what's of ultimate importance to you.

3/ BELIEFS and STRESS

You become what you believe

Rothchild Named Outstanding Citizen

"...Claudia Rothchild is a human dynamo, an energetic, well-organized, multi-talented woman. President of the League of Women Voters, trustee of Community Hospital, she's still found time to organize a volunteer remedial reading program at Jefferson Elementary School. The mother of three children, she devotes the same kind of enthusiastic energy to her family that she's always put into community services. Balancing so many projects, she never shows a sign of wear and tear. Surely, if anyone has learned how to both give and get the most out of life, it's Claudia."

So went the closing paragraph in the Sunday newspaper feature lauding Claudia's civic accomplishments.

"Paul, you've spent all afternoon in front of that television set, just watching football. You've got to get ready. We have company coming at 7:00!"

"Aw, get off me. It's only 5:30. Why don't you sit down and relax for once, like a normal person?"

And so went the closing paragraph in the conversation between the human dynamo and her loving husband later that same Sunday.

Claudia is an impressive woman, no doubt about it. Active, vibrant, highly charged. She reads the paper while eating breakfast, takes care of phone calls while washing dishes, prides herself on working well under pressure. Her pet peeves are slow drivers and waiting in line. Her family can find little fault with her, except that she tends to finish their sentences. The only time she's at a loss is when she has nothing to do.

Claudia is vibrant and healthy, but she, too, experiences stress. Her stomach burns when a committee misses a deadline on a project. Her back aches at the end of a particularly hectic day. Sleep often eludes her as she mentally reviews the day.

Claudia might be surprised to discover that both the valued strengths and the costly stress of her success-oriented life style stem from her belief system—her views about the world, herself and what makes life worthwhile.

Why are beliefs so important?

Your beliefs determine the emphasis (you could even call it the "stress"!) you place on various aspects of your life and its different events.

To many people, the word "belief" means religion—Lutheran or Catholic, Jewish or Baha'i. Religious faith is only a part of your belief system—one example of the many beliefs by which we live.

Every action, every choice you make, follows from your beliefs. For example, if you believe people can be trusted and you expect them to come through in a pinch, that belief will make you act—as a parent or a friend or a supervisor—very differently from someone who believes that others cannot be trusted.

Your beliefs are the core of you. They make you unique. No two people ever have exactly the same belief system. They are the source of your strengths, the most precious, private, vulnerable part of you.

What is my belief system?

Your belief system comprises your changing answers to the ultimate questions of life, questions like:
- What is the aim of my life? (Your goals)
- What is important to me? (Your values)
- What do I believe? (Your faith)
- Who am I, anyway? (Your self-concept)

Claudia might reply, ''My goals are to raise a productive, healthy family, to help other people and to live a full, active life. Hard work, my family and 'being on top of things' are most important to me. I believe that anything worth doing is worth doing well. I would feel guilty if I rested on my laurels. I need to feel that I'm successful.''

Like Claudia, your belief system is the ''blueprint'' from which you construct your life style. Since your life style choices determine the types of stressors you will consistently encounter, your beliefs are at the root of your stress habits.

Dealing with $10 problems

You probably haven't spent much time pondering your belief system or examining how it affects your life. That's fine—so long as you don't experience any major life upheavals. You can deal with the 10¢ problems most of the time by changing your perception or using one of your natural coping skills.

To cope with the $10 and $100 life struggles, however, you need to look a bit deeper than individual stressors. You need to examine, evaluate, affirm, discard, reconcile, modify and rediscover those goals, values, beliefs, self-concepts that are of central importance in your life. They're likely to be the underlying source of your distress, because they have guided you as you carved out your life style from the hundreds of choices available to you each day.

If you are experiencing a lot of stress—more than your share of $10 and $100 problems—you may need to examine your beliefs. The first step is to determine exactly what your beliefs are and how they may be causing you stress. Then you can make deliberate decisions to discard certain beliefs and develop others, and you can make clearer choices to invest more of yourself in the aspects of your life that are most important to you.

Let's apply the process to each of the four belief system components.

Goals:

What is the purpose of my life?

Your goals help you decide how you spend your time and energy. Short term goals, such as planting the garden or making a phone call, determine what you will do with your next half hour. Longer term goals, such as losing 30 pounds or achieving financial security, give shape to your more distant future.

Goals are motivators. They give purpose to life and help you select the actions you're willing to take to fulfill them—and yourself.

Some of your goals are probably very concrete and specific: take a weaving course, buy a new refrigerator, clean out the hall closet. Others may be more vague and philosophical: be a good friend, feel better about yourself.

STOP AND REFLECT

• Make a list of your current goals.

FOR TODAY

write my senator _____

_____

_____

(Continued)

THIS WEEK

s.s. committee

THIS YEAR

self-defense class

REST OF MY LIFE

financial independence

Goals can be the source of distress

You may feel distress if you're not spending your time and energy on the goals you say are important. For example, if you say that your goal is to build lasting friendships, but you're always "too busy" when Debbie calls to invite you to a party, expect to feel anxious the next time she calls or lonely when an empty weekend looms ahead.

If you want to excel as student and athlete, orchestra member and part-time librarian, you're bound to feel frustrated when you can't wear all those hats at once. Having too many goals or conflicting goals is certain to cause you distress.

If you don't know what your goals are, you may move from one meaningless task to another or make sloppy decisions by default. The vague uneasiness you may feel is a symptom of your aimlessness.

Some of Claudia's stress is due to the excessive number of goals she sets for herself. How do your goals, or lack of them, cause you distress?

STOP AND REFLECT

- Which of your goals are suffering because you're not spending enough time and energy pursuing them?

  <u>learning concertina, planting the garden</u>

  _____

  _____

- What goal conflicts are causing you distress?

  <u>independence vs. commitment to family</u>

  _____

- Is having too many goals a problem for you? How about too few?

  _____

Values:

What is important to me?

Your values define what is important in your life—your top priorities. Like goals, they can be measured to some extent by the energy you invest in fulfilling them.

Your values may be more difficult to identify than your goals.

Values work under the surface, propelling you to act, to make choices and to move toward your goals.

When you examine your actions closely, you may discover what you really value. Also, when you examine your values closely, you may understand why you behave the way you do. Values and actions are inseparable. Consider these examples.

If you faithfully report all your income at tax time, you might conclude that you value honesty. If you consistently curl up inside the house with a good book rather than head for the woods, you probably value intellectual stimulation more than outdoor recreation. Generally your actions reflect your values.

If you value privacy, it's no wonder you resent the intrusion of phone calls, or bristle when someone asks you "personal" questions. Values are powerful motivators to action.

What are some of the top priorities in your life?

STOP AND REFLECT

- What values do you hold dear?

1. loyalty
2. competence
3. self-sacrifice
4. _____
5. _____
6. _____

- How do you express those values in your actions?

1. don't betray confidences
2. do what I do well
3. put other's needs first
4. _____
5. _____
6. _____

Values are stressors, too

Values can cause distress when you don't act on them. If you say you value good music and spend your money on hockey tickets instead of the symphony, you're not spending your time and energy in activities you say you value. That's bound to be distressing.

So also, you'll have trouble if two or more of your values are in conflict. If you value both good nutrition and the convenience of fast-food meals, you may suffer from the daily "what shall I do about dinner" dilemma. Conflict usually causes discomfort.

Sometimes you may not even know what your values are. If you find yourself vehemently defending an issue for some "unknown" reason, or if you feel chronically disappointed, the cause of your behavior and feelings probably is that you're out of touch with your underlying values.

Claudia is certainly spending much of her energy on her stated values—hard work, family, success. Some of her distress, though, results from these same values and the conflicts they create.

How might your values be causing some of your distress?

STOP AND REFLECT

- Where in your life are you not acting on your values?

  _____

  _____

- What values conflicts do you experience?

  __honesty_____ and __tactfulness_____

  _____ and _____

  _____ and _____

- With what values might you be out of touch?

  _____

  _____

Faith:

What do I believe?

Everyone has faith in something—God, self, money, evil, the Golden Rule, Walter Cronkite. Faith helps you deal with the ambiguities and mysteries of life. It fills the gaps in your information system.

From an early age, you begin to formulate your faith, that which you choose to define as true for you. Like your room in the house where you grew up, those beliefs become comfortable and familiar. They help you make sense of the world around you.

Your actions are based in part on your faith. If you believe God has a plan for the world and your life, you may face adversity with confidence and trust. If you believe that you are your brother's or sister's keeper, you will look for opportunities to lend a helping hand. If you assume others will be inconsiderate, you will concentrate on protecting yourself. If you believe in forgiveness, you will be more gentle with yourself and others when you or they make mistakes or fail to measure up.

Faith is a central component of your belief system. What do you believe?

STOP AND REFLECT

• What do you believe? Fill in your first reactions to the sentence fragments below.

I believe that people are:

hostile, Trustworthy

_____

_____

_____

(Continued)

I believe that life is:

purposeful, painful

_____

_____

_____

I believe that my stress is:

overwhelming

_____

_____

_____

I believe the world is:

running out of resources

_____

_____

_____

Faith can be a stressor

Your faith may be another underlying source of distress for you, if your beliefs are irrational. For example, if you believe that failure is catastrophic, you may escalate minor troubles into major crises or you may expend much of your energy trying to be "perfect." If you believe that life should always be fun, you'll probably face intense disillusionment in your first job. In both cases irrational beliefs are at the root of your distress.

Holding on to outdated beliefs is also stressful. If you learned as a child, "Don't talk to strangers!" and you still believe the admonition, you'll really be stuck when your seatmate on the subway tries to strike up a conversation.

Claudia clings to the adage, "Anything worth doing is worth

doing well,'' and has trouble being satisfied with a less than perfect job from herself or others—guaranteed instant heartburn.

STOP AND REFLECT

- What's your favorite irrational belief? ''I believe that

_____ ''

- How does that belief cause you distress? _____

_____

Think back to your childhood:

- What were some of the favorite sayings, mottos or slogans of your family?

- What is the belief message of each motto?

- How is that belief still active in your life today?

MOTTO

"Idle hands are the devil's workshop"

_____

_____

BELIEF

my worth is in work

_____

_____

ACTIVE TODAY

project after project

_____

_____

Self-Concept:

Who am I, really?

Your self-concept is a special collection of assumptions and beliefs—beliefs about your limitations, your abilities, your appearance, your emotional resources, your place in the world, your potential, your worthiness.

These self-views, which were primarily learned in childhood and later reinforced through accumulated experience, give continuity to your life, providing a framework from which to respond appropriately to the multitude of choices you face daily.

Self-concept is based on belief rather than objective fact. Your self-image does not necessarily correspond with external reality. You may believe that your hair is your crowning glory, while others like your smile or appreciate your delicate skin.

You may believe that you are creative, lazy, attractive, stubborn, loving, dense, or trustworthy. Whatever you believe about yourself is "true" for you and will be a powerful determiner of your actions. If you believe you are inferior to others, you'll probably tend to defeat yourself. If you believe that you're strong and resilient, you will probably succeed in most undertakings, even against great odds. Beliefs are potent motivators.

How do you view yourself? Depending on its content, your self-concept can either help or hinder you.

STOP AND REFLECT

- Who are you?

  (I believe) I am _friendly, persistent_

  (I believe) I am _____

  (I believe) I am _____

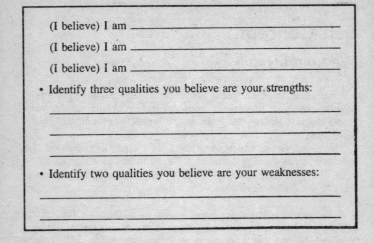

(I believe) I am _____

(I believe) I am _____

(I believe) I am _____

• Identify three qualities you believe are your strengths:

_____

_____

_____

• Identify two qualities you believe are your weaknesses:

_____

_____

When does self-concept cause distress?

Most people cling tenaciously to their odd collection of beliefs about themselves, even when the facts and feedback from others contradict their self-concept. Whenever your self-image is out of whack with external reality, it's bound to cause you distress.

If your self-concept is too rigid, you will discount feedback from others. For example, if you cling to a belief that you are "stupid", you will reject the gift of respect from others who value your ideas and opinions.

Beliefs change very slowly. So does your self-concept. When you hold to an outdated self-concept, you are more vulnerable to distress. Even after losing weight you may have a "fat" self-concept and may therefore deflect the compliments and admiring glances that come your way. The stress of the empty nest syndrome often results from a sluggish self-concept.

Your self-concept may also stop you from realizing your fullest potential. If you believe you can't run a mile, you probably won't try. If you believe you're less qualified than some other candidates, you may not even interview for a job.

STOP AND REFLECT

Look back at your answers to the question, "Who am I?"
• Are any of your self-concept beliefs out of date? _____
_____

• Which of your central self-beliefs do you hold on to rigidly, even in the face of contradictory feedback?
_____
_____
_____

• How do your self-concept beliefs keep you from reaching your fullest potential?

BELIEF

"I don't speak well in public"
_____
_____
_____

HOW IT HOLDS ME BACK

I refuse leadership positions
_____
_____
_____

Summing up

Just as our belief systems support us, so also they can cause distress. Now that you've identified the major components in your belief system, it's time to look at the broader picture. What is the connection between your stress habits and your beliefs?

STOP AND REFLECT

Look back at your answers to the worksheets in this chapter
on values, goals, beliefs and self-concept.
- What basic themes and core issues do you find reflected in
  your answers?

  _____

  _____

  _____

  _____

- How might these belief system issues be related to the stress
  you experience?

  _____

  _____

  _____

  _____

Commitment/ Surrender:

How do I spend myself?

Commitment is your belief system in action.

You can't spend the same quarter twice. You can't be two places
at once or invest yourself wholeheartedly in too many projects or
relationships.

Commitment is your decision to invest yourself. How you spend
your time, where you direct your energy, how much of yourself you
invest—these commitment choices are guided by your goals, values,
beliefs and self-concept. You can be committed to an idea, to a
person, to a fantasy, to a career, to a cause, to a routine or to an
institution. The world is eagerly waiting to absorb all the time and
energy you're willing to spend.

If you're committed to your career and parenting responsibilities, to a governor's commission, to Kiwanis, to exercising an hour a day, to sleeping eight hours and to spending time with your partner, stop reading right now and reserve yourself a room at the nearest hospital. You may need it. You're over-committed—which really means not being committed enough to choose one option over another.

The key to commitment is choice.

Surrender is the flip side of commitment. The limits on your time and energy dictate that when you say "yes" to one option, you may have to say "no" to another.

Surrender may be as simple as adjusting your pace to that of your walking partner, or it may mean postponing or abandoning your own desires for the joy of meeting someone else's needs.

If you tackle every challenge in your path, you may have to be carried away on a stretcher. Refusal to surrender can do you in!

I don't have enough time!

As you listen to the gripes of the people around you, you'll probably notice that one of the most frequently mentioned sources of stress is "not having enough time". This is the chronic complaint of the over-committed and one of Claudia's biggest frustrations.

The truth is that there's no lack of time. You have at your disposal all the time allotted to you. So does Claudia. You can't save time, you can't make more time. But you can and do choose to spend your time in whatever way you wish.

Developing wise spending patterns

There are millions of "want to's" and "have to's" in life. Ultimately, these pressures create stress only when your time and energy spending decisions aren't consistent with your goals, beliefs and values.

What about you? Are your spending patterns in line with your underlying values and beliefs? How are they related to the stress you're currently experiencing?

If the ways you're spending your time and energy aren't bringing

STOP AND REFLECT

• List six major commitments in your life right now:

  finishing my degree, relationship with Mary,
  non-violence
  _____

  _____

  _____

  _____

  _____

• What other commitments would you like to make?

  _____

  _____

  _____

• What present involvements do you need to surrender?

  _____

  _____

  _____

  _____

  _____

• Where in your life have you already consciously made a
  choice to surrender?

  _____

  _____

  _____

  _____

you the rewards you seek, examine your belief system, and in the light of your goals and values make some clear commitment/surrender decisions. This action will automatically reduce your stress. If you're distressed because you don't have enough time, use your goals, beliefs and values to help you cut down on the demands by saying "yes" to some possibilities and "no" to others.

What now?

You've seen how your perceptions and your basic beliefs about yourself and your world orchestrate your response to potentially stressful events in your life.

In the next four chapters we'll help you take a look at four processes that prove particularly stressful for most people: the pace of change in your life, your growth through life's stages, your response to loss and your personal life rhythm.

4/ STRESS and CHANGE

Regulating the rate of change in your life

Your neighbor moves, the cost of living rises, Laura gets chicken pox, the corner grocery closes, you fall in love, your father has a heart attack, the pool is closed for cleaning, you rearrange the living room, you start eating sprouts, wingtips go out of style, your evening class is canceled, there's a detour on the way to work, Aunt Myrtle moves out of her apartment, the hot water heater springs a leak, WSCD goes country.

Change is unavoidable.

Sometimes the cause of change is external: a new job, the breakup of a family or a car accident. Sometimes it's internal: revised goals or new feelings.

Why is change so stressful?

Whatever the source, change is stressful by its very nature. Changes call upon you to adapt, and any adaptation stresses your body systems.

When too many changes occur too fast, you put excessive strain on yourself. As you struggle to adapt, you may feel depressed, get physically sick or make foolish decisions.

Research into the relationships between life change, stress and health supports the idea that change takes its toll. Four areas emerge as central in understanding the connection between stress and change.

An accumulation of changes over time or a large number of changes in a brief period increases stress—and your risk

of physical illness. If you move this year—changing living arrangements, jobs, churches, friends, financial status, climate—you'll subject yourself to a stress overload that will make you three times more likely to experience an illness or accident during the coming year than your neighbor who made few life changes.

Both positive and negative changes are stressful. Both call for system-wide adaptation. A promotion can be just as stressful as a demotion.

Changes tend to come in clusters, creating their own momentum. One change leads to another. The stress also escalates, of course, as one adaptation demands another.

Some life changes consistently cause more stress than others. The death of a young child is more stressful than a financial reversal, a divorce more stressful than a change in jobs.

What changes are more stressful?

Although researchers have not yet pinned down the dynamics of the relationship between belief systems and stress, it is easy to see that such a correlation exists. The changes that cause the most stress are those which threaten what's most important to you. Normally, losing a mate will cause the highest degree of stress, but if you're married to your work, losing your job may put you under greater stress than losing your husband or wife. If physical ability is very important to you, a disabling accident may cause you far more stress than it would to someone who cares mostly about intellectual ability. It takes more energy to adapt to changes that challenge what you hold most dear.

How about you? What changes have disrupted the pattern of your life recently?

STOP AND REFLECT

Check the life changes you have experienced this year:

PERSONAL

—— personal injury/illness, handicap
—— pregnancy (yours or partner's)
—— change in religious views/beliefs
—— change in financial status
—— change in self-concept
—— ending a relationship
—— change in emotional outlook
—— change in roles
—— buying/selling a car
—— aging
—— change in habits
　—— alcohol
　—— drugs
　—— tobacco
　—— exercise
　—— nutrition

WORK

—— changed work load
—— change in pay
—— starting new job
—— promotion/demotion
—— retirement
—— change in hours
—— change in relationships at work
—— change in job security
—— strike
—— change in financial status

FAMILY

—— marriage
—— family member(s) leaving home
—— new family member(s)
—— separation/divorce

(Continued)

—— trouble with in-laws
—— partner stopping/starting a job
—— illness/healing of family member
—— death of close friend or family member
—— parent/child tensions
—— change in recreation patterns

ENVIRONMENT

—— natural disaster
—— moving to new:
  —— house or apartment
  —— neighborhood
  —— city
  —— climate
  —— culture
—— Christmas
—— vacation
—— remodeling
—— war
• major house cleaning
• crime against property

• Go back and mark the changes that required extra adaptation because of their importance to you.
• Identify one change that had a surprising effect on you: ___

_____

• How did it affect you? _____

_____

Should I try to prevent change?

Change isn't necessarily bad. In addition to adding zest to life, change provides an opportunity to test your values and beliefs in new situations and to keep your adaptation skills in good working order.

It might seem that the fewer changes you experience, the less stress you'll be under and the less likely you are to become ill. Not true.

People who undergo too **few** life changes experience stress-related problems, too. They often find their energy level dropping. They may become dispirited, lose their capacity to love and fall prey to a host of physical symptoms. Their sense of worth may diminish. Life without stimulation, challenge and meaning bores most folks.

It's all a matter of degree. You need to arrive at your own proper balance between too much and too little. Your optimum level of change will stimulate without overwhelming you. A healthy balance will enhance rather than diminish your physical energy, your emotional stability, your ability to love and your capacity for hope.

STOP AND REFLECT

- How much change are you experiencing right now?
  - —— too little change
  - —— too much change
  - —— crisis: going bananas
  - —— just the right amount of change

- What distress are you experiencing from that level and pace of change? _____
  _____
  _____
  _____
  _____

Regulating the momentum of change

Although the world around you is moving at a pace you cannot control, you can alter the momentum of change in your life.

What if you're moving too slowly? If your life is nearly change-less, you could be in danger of stagnating. You may need to embark on new ventures. Learn to say "yes". Don't wait to be asked. Volunteer. If you're dying of boredom, you might even want to experiment with change for the sake of change: eat cereal for supper, put your bed in the living room, talk to a stranger, paint your bathroom purple. While you're waiting for the momentum of change to build up steam in your life, lay some groundwork. Sign up for a night course to prepare yourself for a more interesting job. Join a dancing class.

What if you're changing too rapidly? If you find that you're going too fast, that the stress is too great and you need to cut down on the pace of change in your life, you will want to exercise the skill of saying "no". Shut some doors. Relinquish some of the options. Forget the guilt trip. Do only what is absolutely essential. Slacken your pace by saying "no" to non-essentials until you have assimi-lated the changes you've already endured.

What if your life goes bananas? If you find that the pace of change in your life is causing a major crisis, what you need is a survival strategy. When your life is falling apart, you don't need intricate plans for improving it. Just **hold on**—hang on to whatever will help you get through the week, the day, the next hour. A trusted friend or family member, your religious faith, a treasured book, a tranquilizer, old love letters—lean on any resource that might sup-port you through the crisis. Now is **not** the time for major repairs. Wait until your life settles down again.

What if your change rate seems just right? Take notes! Enjoy! Remember what it feels like so you'll know the equilibrium to strive for the next time the balance is tipped. And it's bound to tip again at some point!

Certain predictable changes related to our personal maturation process put us under special stress from time to time. Chapter 5 explores the changes that typify the various adult life stages.

5/ STRESS and LIFE STAGES

The terrible 2's, 22's, 32's, 42's . . .

What are you going to be when you grow up?

He's struck out and the game is over. Nine-year old Bert tucks his ball glove under his arm and starts trudging home. He sees the paper boy riding by on his bike and thinks: "Wow! When I get to be 12 and have a paper route of my own—then I'll really be something!"

Matt rounds the corner and flings the last paper up on the O'Donnells' porch as Bert goes by. He stares after the little boy for a minute. "Boy, was it nice when all I had to do was play ball with the other kids," he thinks. Then his attention is caught by Kirk, who comes out the door twirling the keys to his new Toyota pickup. "I can hardly wait till I'm 16," Matt says to himself enviously. "I'll buy an old van and really fix it up. All the other kids will sure sit up and take notice then!"

As he peels out, Kirk pounds his fist on the steering wheel and mutters under his breath: "Don't drive too fast. Be home by 10. Brother! Just wait till I get into college like Doug. Then I can do what I want, when I want, with nobody running my life for me."

Doug is holed up in the university library, studying for final exams. "College days sure have been fun," he thinks. "The time the fraternity filled all the salt shakers with sugar. The time I saved the day with that impossible touchdown pass and the team carried me off the field on their shoulders. The time I helped Maggie crawl in through a window when she lost her keys. Ah, yes—Maggie." Doug's thoughts slip easily to his bouncy, brown-haired fiancee.

"Gee, I can hardly wait to get out of here so we can get married. Shoot—Mom and Dad were married and had me by the time they were my age! Sure would beat all this booking."

Mom breathes a sigh of relief as she piles the last load of laundry into the dryer. *"I can hardly wait until all the kids are out of the house, and I can do what I want again. Liz is so lucky. She packed the last kid off to college and went back to nursing school herself. Now she can really make a contribution."* She looks around her kitchen and sighs. *"I sure wish Maggie and Doug weren't so eager to get married. I remember when I was Maggie's age. If I hadn't already been tied to a house and baby, I could have finished school. Pursued my dancing career. Maybe even gone to Europe. There are so many possibilities when you're young."*

Mrs. Humphreys interrupts Mom's reverie. *"Hallo-o-o! Anybody home?"* she calls. Mom hurries out the back door to help her 70-year-old neighbor up the steps. *"You're young and spry, just like I used to be,"* Mrs. Humphreys puffs as she hobbles into the kitchen and sits down. *"You don't know how lucky you are. The arthritis has got me so bad I can hardly walk anymore. But my doctor's trying a new treatment. If it works, I can take care of myself instead of moving in with my daughter, like she wants me to. I don't want to live there. That household's too hectic for me."*

Bert, Matt, Kirk, Doug, Maggie, Mom, Liz and Mrs. Humphreys—all share something in common. They are experiencing one of the normal, predictable stages of human development—and yearning to get on to the next stage or trying to hold on to one that's passed.

We all have fantasies of "getting it together" in the next stage of life, and we all also feel the need to hang on to "the good old days".

Life stages are natural and stressful

From the "terrible twos" to the "sentimental seventies", everyone goes through life stages. It's part of the normal growth process. Adult development, like that of children, occurs in a predictable, if not always orderly, pattern. Bodies change. Responsibilities shift. Goals are revised. Dreams are restructured. Self-image fluctuates. Change is an inevitable part of growth.

Each life stage poses unique developmental tasks. There are challenges to be met, skills to be developed, issues to be resolved. The young adult must leave the family, establish independence, test values. The older adult needs to accept mortality and personal limitations, nurture deep friendships, deal with grief.

Each life stage has its unique stresses as well. The striving for success after leaving school, the values upheaval of the "mid-life crisis" and the loss of companions that accompanies aging are intrinsically stressful. Adults have "growing pains", too.

The stress of growth is compounded if you fight the process or don't give yourself permission to experience a stage fully. You probably indulge your two-year-old child's rebelliousness, knowing that autonomy is an important issue at that age. Are you as tolerant of yourself when you're in the midst of your own struggle to grow?

The question is not, "Do you grow and change?" or "Should you grow and change?" Growth is inevitable. The question is, "How do you handle the stress of each stage of development to minimize its negative effects and enjoy its maximum benefits?"

STOP AND REFLECT

Use these brief descriptions of the issues commonly encountered in each life stage to see where you are in your own journey. Within the appropriate stages—
- Cross out the issues you've already dealt with.
- Circle the issues that you're struggling with now.

Breaking loose (late teens): Leaving home, focus on peers, testing your wings, loneliness, attachment to causes, changing life style, throwing out family morals, conforming to friends.

Building the nest (twenties): Search for identity, intimate friendships, marriage, intoxication with own power, great dreams, making commitments, taking on responsibilities, getting launched in a career, working toward goals, doing "shoulds", finding a mentor, having children.

(Continued)

Looking around (thirties): Raising questions, recognizing painful limitations, gathering possessions, moving up the career ladder, declining satisfaction in marriage, settling down, desiring freedom, asking "What do I want to do with my life?"

Mid-life rebirth (around forty): Awareness of mortality, diminishing physical energy, emotional turmoil, parenting teenagers, finding new friends, deep questions, changing careers, second adolescence, sense of aloneness, divorce, remarriage, conflicting pressures, remodeling life structure, learning to play again.

Investing in life (fifties): Life reordered, settling down, acting on new values, focus on people instead of possessions and power, selecting a few good friends, last child leaving home, grandparenting, more financial freedom, enjoying life, empty nest, lost dreams.

Deepening wisdom (later years): Softening feelings, mellowing wisdom, steady commitments to self and others, deepening richness, simplifying life, adjustment to limitations, loss of energy, financial pressures, retirement, quiet joys, self-knowledge, self-acceptance, facing death.

Twilight years: Loneliness, freedom from "shoulds", dependence on those who once depended on you, mind sharp/body failing, body fine/mind failing, loss of mate and friends, preparing for death, sense of peace and perspective.

• In what stage of adult development are you right now?

_____

• How are you experiencing changes in yourself physically (energy, sexuality, general health, etc.)?

_____

_____

_____

(*Continued*)

- Describe changes in your self-image and the direction you're headed. _____

_____

- Describe changes in your relationships (marriage, family, friends, community). _____

_____

_____

- How has the meaning of your work changed? _____

_____

- What special difficulties are you experiencing in your present stage of development (accidents, disease, emotional problems, family difficulties)? _____

_____

_____

- What observations strike you as you look at your past development and current life stage issues?

_____

_____

- How are these issues contributing to your current stress?

_____

_____

_____

The developmental process is often confusing, difficult, painful. You don't always have good models from whom to learn. You may feel as if you're fumbling along all your life, trying to "grow up". Changes often happen before you're ready for them, and you don't always have the skills needed to meet the new demands. There's no way around it. Growth is stressful.

You can add to your stress

But you can make it even worse. You can increase the stress of the natural process if you aren't aware of what's going on, if you fight it instead of accepting it.

You can plague yourself by trying to move on to the next stage before you're ready, before you've learned the skills, resolved the issues, completed the tasks of the stage you're in.

You can cling to the past. If you refuse to surrender the security of an outgrown stage, you can't take advantage of the promise of the present one.

You can try to use the same old coping skills at every stage of your life. But at some point they may lose their effectiveness. New challenges often call for new styles, new skills.

You can conclude that you're "crazy" and berate yourself bitterly, instead of accepting yourself wherever you are and understanding that it's a natural stage.

You can pressure those you love to "grow up". People move through their life stages at different rates of speed. Don't expect yourself and your partner or friends to grow at exactly the same rate.

Travel tips

How can you cope while you're growing through the life stages? Here are a few tips for a smoother journey.

Check your attitude. The natural life stages occur whether you seek them or not. What you make of them is your choice. Periodically assess your attitude. Are you viewing the transition periods as crises or as opportunities for growth?

Identify the stages in your life. Since days and years tend to blend together, it may take some effort for you to see the signposts of your development. Periodically write notes to yourself about your goals, your feelings, your commitments. Read them regularly, perhaps on your birthday. They'll give you a clear picture of where you've been.

Cultivate deep friendships. Be sure to include people both younger and older than yourself. Take time for intimate conversation and reflection with friends. Ask meaningful questions. Listen to each other as you share the experiences of growth.

Dress yourself in a new wardrobe of coping behaviors. Some techniques that worked in earlier stages won't be effective when you're older. Update your repertoire. Each stage of life demands the selection of coping mechanisms appropriate to the problems of that period.

Don't take yourself too seriously. When you feel desperate and can't find your path through a trying period, you have a perfect excuse. "It's only a stage."

Don't try to figure it all out ahead of time. Remind yourself that "When the student is ready, the teacher appears."

Trust the process

Growing older is not a downhill process from 17 to 70. It's an unfolding, like the maturing of a rose. The bud holds a promise in its tightly formed compactness but has not yet achieved its full beauty. The maturing rose opens petal by petal, facing greater and greater risk as it becomes exposed. Previously unseen potential becomes visible. As the process continues, each new layer of petals unfolding adds depth and significance to the flower.

So also with you—your potential unfolds as you age. In the bud of life, only a portion of your loveliness shows. Your potential is revealed in the unfolding process. Each stage reveals new beauty. Each stage brings fuller life. Each stage allows a more complete expression of your inner self.

No birth takes place without pain. No rebirth takes place without death. No new life is created without burying some of the old.

The quality of your journey through life and its stages is determined primarily by your attitude. Life's turning points are times of high risk, great stress—occasions for opportunity and exciting potential. You choose whether your movement through life's stages is a delight or a disaster.

Growing up usually means giving up some of what we cherished in the stage just past. The stress that accompanies that letting-go process is similar in kind, if not intensity, to grief—the process of healing from a loss. Chapter 6 takes a closer look at the special stress of the grieving person.

6/ Stress and Grief

It's tough to let go

What is grief?

Grief is the process of healing from the pain of loss.

If you've ever had to say good-bye—to a friend or spouse, to an image of yourself or a glorious dream, to a special possession—then you've experienced grief. The term "grief" applies not only to the desperate, sad, empty feelings connected with the death of someone close, but also to the scaled-down versions of these feelings that accompany the smaller disappointments and losses of daily living.

Over a lifetime you relinquish a host of life's treasures—small pearls like an afternoon at the beach, valuable jewels like a cherished relationship with a grandparent. Letting go of such treasures involves pain. The pain of a parent's death is more overwhelming than the disappointment of a canceled vacation. But the fact is, both losses hurt. The death of a relative, the death of a pet, the death of a dream—all set grief into motion.

STOP AND REFLECT

• Recall a variety of loss experiences in your life. List some of your major griefs and some minor, everyday losses.

MAJOR LOSSES

Mort's move , grandpa's stroke

_____

_____

_____

(Continued)

MINOR LOSSES

didn't get the job offer, breaking my special teapot

What can I expect from the grief process?

When you lose something important to you, your entire life is affected. You grieve with your whole being, not just your mind or body or spirit.

Most people move through a series of stages when they're grieving, steps that help them bid farewell to the past and invest themselves again in the present. The steps don't always occur in sequence, but in one way or another they usually touch your life. The process is as natural and predictable as the formation of a scab on a cut and the subsequent itching sensation that signals healing.

What are the stages?

Shock and denial. Shock is the natural anesthesia of the human emotional system. When the pain is too great, your system temporarily "blows out". You may feel so numb that you act as if nothing had happened.

Emotions erupt. Your emotions break out with wrenching sobs, gentle tears or deep sighs as you suddenly become aware of your painful loss.

Anger. At some point you'll probably feel angry. Angry at God. Angry at the "unfairness" of your loss. Even angry at who or what you've lost for "deserting" you.

Illness. Don't be surprised if physical illness follows a loss experience. Your body may respond to the loss by temporarily breaking down.

Panic. While you're grieving, you won't always feel like your "old self". You may panic and wonder if you're losing your mind. Fortunately, this panic soon diminishes if you don't fight it.

Guilt. In order to endure your pain, you may take personal responsibility for the loss. Feeling guilty often seems more bearable than having no culprit, no explanation.

Depression and loneliness. You may find yourself withdrawing from others who "don't understand". Feelings of isolation, hurt and sadness may escalate into depression.

Re-entry difficulties. You may resist letting go of your attachment to the past and have trouble moving on in life. Loyalty to a memory may delay your return to normal activities.

Hope. Against all odds, somehow hope always sneaks through the cracks, takes root and begins to grow again.

Affirming reality. You reconstruct your life, using the new strengths you've gained from grieving. Death gives way to resurrection.

STOP AND REFLECT

Select one of your losses to probe further: _____
                                                    my loss
Use the chart below to explore the grieving process as it relates to that loss.

• Circle the stages you clearly remember experiencing.
• Cross out the stages you don't remember experiencing.

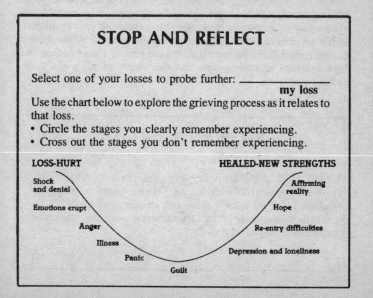

LOSS-HURT   HEALED-NEW STRENGTHS

Shock   Affirming
and denial   reality

Emotions erupt   Hope

    Anger   Re-entry difficulties

     Illness   Depression and loneliness

        Panic

              Guilt

When does grief cause trouble?

Grief is never easy. Few people relinquish their treasures gladly. Few enjoy the painful feelings that come with loss. Most find it hard to allow healing to proceed at its own pace. Yet resisting the natural progression of grief is bound to cause trouble.

If you short-circuit the healing process by refusing to acknowledge your suffering, you will compound your distress. When you adopt coping methods designed to hide your feelings and numb your pain, you delay the process of healing. The wound festers beneath the surface only to erupt later—even years later—with greater intensity.

Getting stuck in the grieving process can also create an added measure of destructive stress. If you're stuck in shock, you may lose touch with reality, like the widow who still sets a plate at the dinner table for her dead husband. If you don't deal with guilt, you may erode your sense of self-esteem, like the father who eventually shot himself five years after his son was killed on the motorcycle that he had given his son for Christmas.

You can be immobilized in any one of the grief stages—perpetual panic, recurring illness, unrelenting depression—sometimes without even knowing that unresolved grief is the source of your symptoms.

It's possible to get stuck and stay stuck for years. Fortunately, few people remain stuck forever. Usually, the healing nature of time, the love and care of other people and the variety of life's challenges prod us gently on.

STOP AND REFLECT

Look back at the chart of your grief process. What stages were especially difficult for you? These might be stages in which you "got stuck" or are still stuck.
• List below those stuck stages along with the particular symptoms you experienced.

(Continued)

STAGE

re-entry difficulties

SYMPTOMS

too much TV, no outings

• What strategies have you used or could you use to free yourself from being stuck?

Most people who are grieving don't need psychotherapy. Most don't need medication either, although it can be helpful in small amounts for brief periods of time. What grieving people need most is the courage to let go, the faith that they will heal and the willingness to rejoin life fully.

What about you? Do you think any of your physical problems are caused by your refusal to release your hold on lost treasures? Is any of your anger an unwillingness to say good-bye? Could any of your depression be the result of clinging to an old image of yourself? Is any of **your** stress caused by unresolved grief?

STOP AND REFLECT

- What distress that you're currently experiencing might be a
  symptom of being stuck in the grieving process? What loss
  are you grieving?

SYMPTOMS

cynicism, anger

_____

_____

_____

_____

LOSS

Jeanne's illness

_____

_____

_____

_____

What do I do about grief?

By all means, go ahead and grieve! Grief is not the problem; it's
the solution.

Give yourself permission to grieve. People who undergo surgery
generally anticipate some pain and accept the fact that they won't
regain full physical strength for quite some time. People rarely make
the same allowances for the "surgery" of a severe emotional loss.
They often don't allow themselves the time it takes to heal, com-
pounding their stress by becoming impatient. Give yourself permis-

sion to feel the pain that naturally follows loss. Take time to recover.

Invest yourself again. To finish grieving you must make new investments. Look for people and situations in which you can invest your love and energy.

Allow your faith to mature. Loss reminds us of life's impermanence. Every grief experience invites you to renew your acquaintance with life's mysteries and to reaffirm your faith, even in light of your loss.

Lean on others. Share your grief with others—it keeps the healing process flowing. Join a group of people who are each working through their own grief process and who are committed to caring. Sometimes you can't do it alone. Reach out.

When do I get over it?

You don't.

The rainbow hues of your grief—the red-yellow anguish, the blue-green questions, the purple confidence—are woven permanently into the tapestry of your life. By the time the healing process is finished and your loss is fully assimilated, you will have shuttled back and forth through all the stages of grief, shaping an unlikely masterpiece of life from death, creating love and commitment from the pain of letting go.

The grieving process always alters the mourner. Grief invariably leads to new strengths: When you allow yourself to experience fully the subtle gradations of its colors and textures, grief adds to your personal richness and depth.

Just as there is a pattern and a pace to grief, there is a natural rhythm to all of life. Living out of step with that rhythm is stressful. In the next chapter you'll examine the stress of being out of step with your natural rhythm.

7/ STRESS and LIFE RHYTHM

Marching to your own drummer

What's my rhythm?

The natural world is full of rhythm. The sun rises and sets. The seasons change. The tides ebb and flow. The seven-year locusts return.

You have a natural rhythm, too—daily or hourly patterns, weekly or monthly ups and downs, times to plunge ahead and times to sit back and assimilate. Physical energy, emotional potency, intellectual curiosity, sociability, productivity, moods—all come and go in cycles.

Have you ever felt as if you're out of step with the beat of your life, marching to someone else's rhythm, one step ahead or one step behind your own?

Most people are out of touch with their natural rhythm. Awakened by alarm clocks, eating lunch when their supervisor tells them to, hurrying to finish school, visiting Mother on Sunday afternoon, their natural rhythm is interrupted.

Most people find that speeding up or slowing down their own natural rhythm disturbs their balance and creates tension.

Stop for a moment

Try to become aware of your own rhythm. Stand up and start moving in some way (walking, swaying, stretching, bending) till you find a style and pace that feels natural, comfortable, familiar. Really tune in to yourself. Do what feels good. Pay attention to your heartbeat, your breathing, your muscle tone, your sense of balance.

Now, speed up your movement a little bit, then more dramatically. Be aware of how this hurried pace feels.

Return to your natural rhythm. See how that feels in comparison.

Then slow your pace way down. Be aware of how this slowdown affects your breathing, your balance, your heartbeat.

Why listen to my rhythm?

Resisting your natural rhythm takes a lot more energy than going with its cadence.

Responding to your own rhythm takes self-awareness and practice. You have to pay attention to your own signals and adjust your external pace to match your internal rhythm.

It's worth the effort. Who wants to be a turtle chasing a car?

You can't get in touch with your rhythm if you're holding yourself rigid. You can't dance life's dance if you don't relax. Even the vibrating beds in roadside motels will give you nothing but a 25¢ headache if you can't let go and move with the purr of the motor. You won't get your quarter's worth out of life either, if you don't learn to let go and flow with your own rhythm.

Flowing with life's ups and downs is not nearly as exhausting as a perpetual struggle against the pulse. If you drive your new car pell-mell up the Alaskan Highway, within 1,500 miles a brand-new machine will be worn out. One bump doesn't do it. Hundreds of thousands do. Charging over the bumps turns a car into a prematurely discarded collection of loose connections and broken parts. So it is with life. Crash-banging over life's bumpy road, a journey made rougher by unplanned stops and starts, sudden turns and wild fluctuations in speed, eventually will bring even the healthiest person to a screeching halt. Drive through your life this way and soon you may find yourself on that great scrap pile down the road before—maybe way before—your time.

STOP AND REFLECT

• How do you normally respond to the rhythm of your life?
—— I'm usually pushing ahead of my own rhythm.
—— I'm usually right in harmony with my own rhythm.
—— I'm usually lagging behind my natural rhythm.

• At this moment I'm _____
    (ahead of, behind, right in step with)
the rhythm of my life.

Getting back in step

If you're at odds with the rhythm of your life, you can get back in step by following three basic principles.

Pay attention to your internal rhythm. If you're a "charger", always going full bore and forcing yourself to accomplish too much too quickly, then your task is to learn to throttle back to your natural rhythm rather than scrambling to stay ahead of yourself. Your challenge is to listen to the subtle sounds of life within you and swing along with the cadence of that music. If you're worried about missing the boat, remember the Titanic.

If you're a "lagger" who crawls along, hanging back and procrastinating, then you, too, need to listen. There are "right" moments for bold and daring actions. Seize them and go for it.

Conserve your energy. Just ride along through the jolts and delays of life, instead of fighting them. Why not? Your rhythm will carry you.

Let your rhythm guide your actions. Trust your internal wisdom. Attend to your own needs of the moment. If now is a time to be quiet, be quiet. If it's time for you to fight, then fight. If it's a time to play, play wholeheartedly. You can't make jam till the strawberries are picked.

It's the right time

Have you ever felt the exhilaration of perfect timing: a soaring drive from the tee, a well-timed joke or a business deal that falls smoothly into place? If so, you probably also know the tension of a strained silence, a tennis serve that hurts from wrist to hip, a production schedule doomed to disaster from the beginning, a paragraph that just won't fit. Everyone can feel when the timing is right and when the timing is wrong.

The Greeks used the word "kairos" to describe the "right time" —those magic moments when you are in harmony with your natural rhythm, in tune with the entire universe. The "kairos" may be the right time to plunge wholeheartedly into that church committee, or to spend some extra time with your father, or to re-establish contact with an old friend, or, to start a new business venture.

Listen! Now is your "kairos". Now is the right time for you. The question is, what is it the right time for?

STOP AND REFLECT

Use the questions below to help identify your natural rhythm at this particular time in your life.

• Write down the first thought that enters your mind.

Maybe I don't need to (be/do) _____
(something you need to give up)
any more.

Maybe I still need to (be/do) _____
(something you need to hang on to)
some more.

Maybe I need to (be/do) _____
(a future direction or goal)
sometime soon.

(Continued)

Maybe I need to (be/do) _____
(a past resource or strength to revive)

once again.

Maybe I need to (be/do) _____
(something inconsistent or tentative)

sometimes.

• Look at your answers. What is the "kairos" for you right now?

Now is the right time for me to _____

_____

_____

_____

Answer these questions six or eight times a year. The process will help you get back in touch with your own sense of timing. Your answers will probably differ each time. Why not? Your rhythm itself is always changing.

Now is the time to change the rhythm of this book. In the next chapters you'll be asked to inventory your personal stress management skills and to consider expanding your repertoire of coping methods.

8/ SKILLS for MANAGING STRESS

Identifying coping patterns

"Skills for managing stress?" you may say. "I'm not sure I have any. I just do what comes naturally."

That's the point. "What comes naturally" is your typical coping style—your stress skills. You use coping skills all the time. A coping skill is nothing more than a way of adapting to stress. It doesn't necessarily solve the problem; it simply helps you handle it. It doesn't eliminate the stressor—it helps you manage the stress.

What do you do when someone asks you for "just one more favor"? Throw up your hands in dismay? Say, "No!" Scream and shout? Pout? Bargain by saying, "I'll do this for you if you'll do that for me." Say, "Sure." No matter which response you choose, you're using a stress skill. Screaming, bargaining, throwing up your arms or just throwing up—all are ways of coping, ways of managing stress.

What are some of your customary coping skills?

STOP AND REFLECT

- List several ways you typically cope when you feel stressed.

  crying, eating, hot baths, exercise

  _____

  _____

  _____

How did I develop my coping skills?

Although these behaviors come "naturally" to you now, they were once as unfamiliar as skydiving to some or knitting to others. You had to learn them and practice them before you honed them into the skills you now take for granted.

Where did you learn them?

The process of skill-building really began with your first breath! You learned by observation. By trial and error. By trial and success.

At 10 Bruce was praised, perhaps even paid, when he cleaned his room or helped Dad mow the grass. At 20 he made the honor roll, got pats on the back from home and juicy job offers when he earned good grades and made a name for himself in athletics. At 30 he's busy climbing the career ladder, his efforts rewarded by promotions and pay raises.

"Accomplishing something" is one of Bruce's natural coping skills.

As a child, when she felt unhappy, Ellen went off by herself and sat on the riverbank with a fishing pole, daydreaming. At 20 she hopped in her car and took a long drive. At 30 she jogs, not just for the exercise, but for the time it gives her to be alone.

"Getting away from it all" is one of Ellen's natural stress skills.

STOP AND REFLECT

Your responses to the situations described below will show you how your coping skills developed. Don't deliberate. Jot down the first thing that comes to mind.

- First, describe what your typical response would be today.

- Then try to remember how you would have responded as a child and as a young adult.

(Continued)

SITUATION: When you really mess something up

- Today I typically _berate myself, worry about it_
- As a child I would have _cried, felt guilty_
- As a young adult I would have _denied it, felt guilty_

SITUATION: When someone tells you "no"

- Today I typically _____
- As a child I would have _____
- As a young adult I would have _____

SITUATION: When you're feeling "empty"

- Today I typically _____
- As a child I would have _____
- As a young adult I _____

SITUATION: When you're really angry with someone you care about

- Today I typically _____
- As a child I would have _____
- As a young adult I _____

Look over your answers.

- What are your two or three favorite coping techniques?

_____

_____

_____

- In what ways are you still using your childhood coping style?

_____

_____

_____

Whether they stem from childhood, adolescence or yesterday's desperation, there's nothing wrong with relying on coping skills that work. The trouble is, sometimes they stop working. Skills get outdated. You get in a rut. Short term measures may be ineffective when stretched over the long haul. Or the price gets too high to pay.

Skills can cost too much

Every coping mechanism has a price and a payoff. Drinking alcohol to unwind is a coping skill. It works. It also costs something: a headache the morning after, loss of productive time and creativity, the irritation and embarrassment your behavior causes others, possible liver damage.

Keeping your mouth shut when you're angry, drinking coffee to stay awake, staying home from work when you have a cold—these and hundreds of other behaviors can be effective stress skills. But each has its price.

Some coping skills are better bargains than others. Some are stop-gap measures. Crying, shouting or taking a bath may get you through a few hours of stress, but they can't be relied on forever. Others, such as regular exercise or talking with friends, yield high profits at a low cost.

Skills can wear out

Once a coping mechanism works for you, you're likely to use it over and over again. It seems easier than trying new ones, less risky. That's why most people end up in ruts. In fact, it can be dangerous to limit your coping repertoire to a few familiar skills that must suffice in almost all situations.

For example, if cat-napping is one of your customary coping strategies, it may work well in church, but not if you're the minister. Dozing off after work is great, but not if you're in the midst of a family conflict.

STOP AND REFLECT

Think about your typical coping strategies.

• Which of your coping skills give you good value for the cost?

crying on Sally's shoulder, swimming, laughter

• Which may be costing you too much?

smoking, shopping!, blowing my top

• What coping ruts are you stuck in? Which skills do you tend to overuse?

organizing everything, reading

• Which of your coping skills are probably outdated?

thumb-sucking, all-nighters

Coping skills can also stop working simply because they're outdated. Some skills which are perfect for one stage in your life won't work at all in another.

If you lifted yourself out of depression by playing championship tennis at age 24, the same coping mechanism isn't going to be as effective at 45. Acting childish may have gotten you what you wanted when you were very young. It may even have worked to some extent for you in adolescence. But acting childish may be damaging to you and to your children when you've become a parent.

The longer you cling to worn-out coping methods, the greater your stress becomes, and the harder it is to change.

Must I give up my old stress skills?

Whether you cry to cope, eat potato chips, take a warm bath, telephone a friend, listen to music, clean your house, gulp Scotch or go jogging, if the strategy you're using is working well for you, then keep it up. There are no right or wrong ways of managing stress.

But there are more options, many more, than you might think. If your old skills are starting to let you down, or if some of them are starting to cost too much, or if you just want to broaden your range of possibilities, you can learn more skills, new tools to manage your stress.

That's what the following four chapters are designed to help you do. The twenty stress skills described in those chapters are far from the only ones. Anything that helps **you** adapt to the stresses **you** feel is a good stress skill for you.

What do I do first?

Take it one step at a time. Changing your habitual ways of coping with stress is the first step. You can't learn new skills until you're willing to break old habits, and breaking habits is difficult. Old habits are like a cozy bed—easy to get into and hard to get out of.

You can help yourself by whittling the task down to a size you can manage. Don't overwhelm yourself by resolving to break all your old habits overnight. Focus instead on developing **one new habit**. If you agree to practice just one new behavior, you'll begin to change.

You also can concentrate on creativity. To revitalize yourself, seek vital solutions. If you've always done it one way, that's the best reason to try it another way. It could give you a whole new perspective on your problem and its management.

What next?

Practice. And be patient with yourself. New skills don't develop overnight. They feel awkward at first. If you've ever learned to ski, you can remember how strange you felt at first—crossed skis, wobbly knees, feet too heavy to lift, aching ankles, falling. Learning to ski takes courage and persistence. You have to hang in there until the movements become familiar and effortless.

Stress skills, like the skill of skiing, take the same kind of courage and persistence. At first you may feel foolish and strange. The new coping skill may not make you feel like you're coping at all. That's normal. A new shoe may feel stiff or tight and it may give you blisters the first few times you wear it. But once you break it in, you'll scarcely know you have it on. So also, walking away from an argument, or talking back, or simply surrendering the problem— whatever you try that's new for you—will take a bit of practice before you feel that it fits you comfortably.

Fortunately, learning new skills is also exhilarating. It's fun to try something new. It's stimulating to experiment, to test yourself, to experience a different kind of success. Before you even become proficient at the skill, you'll probably get enough energy back to have made your attempt worthwhile.

Learning new stress skills may be uncomfortable, but it's also exciting—and worth a good try.

STOP AND REFLECT

- What one skill have you tried in the past but given up because it felt so awkward?

  _____

- What do you think would have happened if you'd stuck with it? _____

  _____

- List two skills you've been successful in learning:

  _____

  _____

So, my options are unlimited?

That's right. In the following chapters on personal management, relationship, outlook and physical stamina skills, you'll find a "starter kit" of possibilities. They're not foolproof remedies for all the stressors of life, nor are they the only options. They are good starting points.

Read with your own needs in mind. Keep asking yourself: "Which strategy do I tend to use first? Do I already have numerous coping skills or only a few? Am I neglecting any of my best skills? Is my skill kit well-balanced or one-sided? Are there other skills that would be fun to try?"

Start skill-building now. Your options are boundless.

9/ PERSONAL MANAGEMENT SKILLS

Strategy #1: Organize yourself

If you want to manage your stress by making better use of your time and energy, you can use the skills of:

- **Valuing**—the art of choosing between alternatives
- **Personal planning**—the art of setting goals
- **Commitment**—the art of investing yourself
- **Time use**—the art of spending your time efficiently
- **Pacing**—the art of regulating your tempo

Anne Jackson under stress

"But Mom, Dan and Terry's mothers always come to watch them play softball on Saturday mornings," Tommy complained.

Anne Jackson felt the familiar tightness in her chest as she tried to make excuses to her pleading eight-year-old son. "You knew when I went to work for Dr. Andrews, I promised I'd work Saturdays. He's only open half a day and he's always so busy with all the people who can't come during the week." She sounded defensive, even to herself.

"You promised you'd spend time with me too," Tommy pouted. "Well, at least you can come Friday nights and watch us practice."

Anne felt things closing in on her. Yesterday the church secretary had called to say they still hadn't been able to find a new leader for the Girl Scout troop she used to lead on Mondays, and next week was registration at the nursing school. She'd be in school both Monday and Friday nights if she signed up. And she so wanted to train to be more than a doctor's receptionist.

The front door slammed. "I'm home, Mom. Is supper ready?" Jennifer shouted. Anne barely choked down a wild scream.

How can Anne cope with her stress?

Could personal management skills help?

There are 24 hours in everyone's day, 365 days in everyone's year. Then why do some people always seem to have plenty of time to get their work done, to play, to visit friends, to care for their homes, to relax, while others race frantically against the clock, never quite able to catch up?

Watch how they budget their time and energy, and you'll have the answer.

Whether your stress is the result of events beyond your control or your failure to take charge of your life, personal management skills can help. They can reduce your stress by helping you learn to spend your time and energy more efficiently and effectively.

Personal management or organizing skills are particularly good for the times when:

- you feel as though your life is out of control;
- there's too much to do and not enough time to do it;
- you're spending too much time on non-essentials;
- you feel out of step with yourself; or
- you're not sure what you want.

Valuing skills help you determine what's important to you.
Planning skills let you turn your values into action plans.
Commitment skills give you ways to make those plans work.
Time-use skills help you cut down on wasted time.
Pacing skills save you energy.

Valuing

Choosing between alternatives

Look at the racks in a clothing store. Turtlenecks, V-necks, shorts, slacks, fur coats, cloth coats, evening gowns and night-gowns. The choices are almost endless. None of them is right or wrong, although they may be right or wrong for you. If you're looking for a dress to wear to your sister's wedding, you'd probably walk right by the bathing suits. If you're heading off on a camping trip, you wouldn't bother looking at silk shirts.

So it is with life. Your choices are just about unlimited. But choosing is stressful. What's a good buy and what isn't? What's worth spending your time on? Your energy?

That depends on what's important to you. Valuing skills can help you identify what's important to you, so you can spend your time and energy wisely.

Valuing in Action

Anne Jackson can shut herself in her bedroom or even lock herself in the bathroom if necessary, and spend five quiet minutes calming down.

Then she can make some lists. On one, she writes down things she likes to do: working in a doctor's office, volunteer work at church, knitting, going on picnics with Tommy and Jennifer.

On another list, things she hates to do: fixing an elaborate supper after she's worked all day, spending her only afternoon off scrubbing the bathroom, sitting in the hot sun watching the kids play softball.

On a third list, she jots down a few of her heroes: Albert Schweitzer, because he was such a humanitarian; Amelia Earhart, because she dared to follow her own star.

And on a fourth list, she summarizes how she spent her day, how much of it was allotted to work, Jennifer, Tommy, the house, friends, church, relaxation.

Practice valuing yourself

Start by doing nothing. Sit quietly for five minutes with no agenda. Wait until your mind feels clear and you feel calm.

Make notes on what's important to you. List the things you like to do, the things you don't like to do, what you wish you could do. Write down the qualities you admire in your heroes and the attributes you dislike in people around you. Name the ways you would like to be like your parents and the ways you would rather be different.

Look at your day. What did you spend time on yesterday? How much time? If someone else looked at your list, what would he or she think you valued most? Least? Do you see any conflict between your values and the way you spend your time?

STOP AND REFLECT

- How clear are your values to you? Mark an X where you fall on the line.

| Very
muddy | Unclear | Fairly
clear | Very
clear |

- How could you use valuing skills to respond to your present stress?

_____

_____

_____

- How would it have been useful last weekend?

_____

_____

_____

Personal planning

The art of setting goals

Do you spend your days acting or reacting? If you want to be the captain of your own ship instead of just letting it be buffeted by the winds and waves, you need a plan.

Planning is the way to put your values into action. Once you're clear about where you want to go, planning skills can help you get there.

Planning involves more than making lists of jobs to be done, although that's a good starting point. Once you've got the lists, you need to rank each item in order of its importance to you. Then group them so they can be tackled efficiently. Finally, you need to allot an appropriate block of time to each task.

Planning in action

When Anne finally unlocks the door and comes out of the bathroom with her handful of lists, she can start using them to plan.

She can see she loves medical work. It's right up there at the top of her list. She also likes volunteer work at church, although she doesn't spend much time at it anymore. She doesn't like being expected to cook and keep house the way she did when Tommy was a baby.

So Anne starts making some decisions. She does want to be a nurse. Within five years she wants to have her R.N., even though right now she can only pursue it part time. During the next six months, she wants to get back into some church work that won't be as time-consuming as the Girl Scout troop. And next week, she plans to advertise for some part-time household help.

As for tonight, she tells a hungry and bewildered Jennifer and Tommy she's taking them out for pizza.

Practice planning yourself

Clarify your life goals. Answer the following questions:

- What do you want to do with the rest of your life?
- Where do you want to be in five years?
- What do you want to make happen in the next six months?
- What specific goal will you achieve next week?

Be as specific as possible. You have to know what target you're aiming at before you can hope to hit it. And update your list every three months, or you'll end up shooting at targets you're not even interested in hitting any more.

Make a daily plan. List all the tasks needing attention today. Rank them and relist them in order of importance. Estimate how long each one will take. Start with the first task and move down the list.

Divide and conquer. Break your big life goals into smaller, more manageable chunks. List 30 or 40 five-minute tasks that are a step, if a small one, toward one of your long-range goals. Every day, without exception, spend five minutes moving toward a life goal. You won't feel you're moving very fast, but five minutes a day adds up to more than a day a year, and in 10 years, you'll have devoted nearly two full weeks to your long-range goals—painlessly.

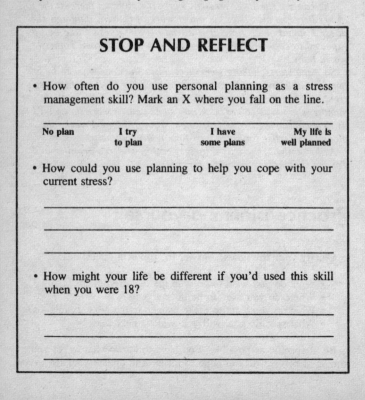

STOP AND REFLECT

• How often do you use personal planning as a stress management skill? Mark an X where you fall on the line.

No plan	I try to plan	I have some plans	My life is well planned

• How could you use planning to help you cope with your current stress?

_____

_____

_____

• How might your life be different if you'd used this skill when you were 18?

_____

_____

_____

Commitment

The art of investing yourself

Ready, set, choose! Commitment is the courageous act of choosing to pursue certain goals and let others go. It's a tough skill to try, because it involves taking chances. You take the plunge and commit yourself. It may bring the rewards you seek, or it may not.

So it's tempting to delay making up your mind. It's easier to let other people, or circumstances, choose for you. Then you're not responsible; you're the poor, innocent victim. Uncommitted. Immobilized—but safe. People who say they're over-committed haven't made up their minds either. They're trying to hold all their options open. Usually they end up frantically trying to do everything until they somehow figure out what's important.

Commitment is a risky business. But the rewards of getting off the fence far outweigh the risks.

Commitment in action

Anne feels ready to make a commitment. She realizes she's been trying to hold all her options open too long.

The very next day, she tells Dr. Andrews: "I can only work half time, starting in two weeks. I'm entering nursing school."

To Tommy and Jennifer she says: "I'm going to work part time and go to nursing school. I'd sure like you to both pitch in and help with the cooking and cleaning. I'll hire someone to clean one day a week, and I promise I'll cook one of my big, old-style dinners on Sundays."

And she tells the church secretary: "I'm sorry, but I can't take the Scout troop back. I still want to help out though. Keep me in mind if you need anything done that I can do at my own convenience, like telephoning or addressing envelopes."

Practice commitment yourself

Make a commitment. Get involved. Take the risk. The steps are. make up your mind; take a step toward your choice; shut off other choices; take the risk; give yourself to it completely.

Volunteer to help. Call someone on the phone today and say, "I want to work." Get involved. Don't wait to be asked.

Build a sense of personal history. Put down roots. Invest yourself in your community. You'll build a sense of belonging that will yield great rewards over the long haul and will help you maintain a perspective on your life.

STOP AND REFLECT

- How good are you at making commitments, at investing yourself? Put an X where you fall on the line.

I'm a fence sitter	I occasionally make commitments	I invest myself readily

- How could commitment help you cope with some stress you face now?

_____

_____

_____

- How was this skill used in 1776?

_____

_____

_____

Time use

Spending your time efficiently

Where did the day go? Where did my vacation go? What happened to my youth?

If you've ever asked questions like those, you know how much stress sloppy time management can cause.

Your use of small scraps of time becomes very significant when you realize that by the time you're 70, you'll have spent an average of 23 years sleeping, 11 years working, 8 years playing, 6 years eating, 5½ years grooming, 3 years being educated, 3 years reading, 3 years talking and 7½ years on odds and ends. Will you feel you've spent it wisely?

If you can cut out just 20 minutes a day of wasted time, by the time you're 70, you'll have gained a whole year.

When you say "I have no time," you're really saying that you aren't managing your time well. You have the same amount of time as everyone else. But you may need to make some management decisions about it.

Time use in action

Looking at her pressure-filled days, Anne can't even imagine how she can find time to fit in the volunteer work she really wants to do for her church. Every minute is filled. She doesn't waste any time.

Or does she? Observing her habits closely for a couple of days, she realizes that she runs a load of wash every morning, even when the machine is barely half full, that she tends to try on three or four outfits before deciding which one to wear, that she watches TV in the evening even when the programs don't interest her.

A load of clothes every other day, a little bit of thought before she reaches into her closet, clicking the TV off when the show doesn't grab her and just like magic, she's gained an hour a day.

Practice time use yourself

Name your time wasters. Don't lie to yourself. What are they? Procrastination? Taking care of the trivia first? Jumping from task to task? Ferret them out, give them pet names and laugh at them when they start to control you.

Start with the biggies. Divide all your tasks into three categories. A's are essential to your life goals. B's are important but not essential. C's are trivia. Do the A's first. Put the C's in a stack on your desk or kitchen counter. Then forget them.

Night or day person? What time of the day are you most alert and creative? Do your A's during that time. Save the B's and C's for the other parts of the day.

Be satisfied with doing a partial job. One expert says 80% of your best work is done during the first 20% of the time you spend. Blast away at your top priorities and let some of the lesser tasks fall by the wayside.

Stop running late. Set your watch five minutes fast. Practice being just a little early.

Check yourself. Keep a time log for a week. How many hours do you spend sleeping, working, driving, with your family, with your friends, being quiet, having fun, etc. Evaluate how you're budgeting your time and adjust it to better match your values, goals and commitments.

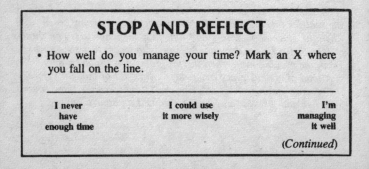

STOP AND REFLECT

- How well do you manage your time? Mark an X where you fall on the line.

I never have enough time	I could use it more wisely	I'm managing it well

(Continued)

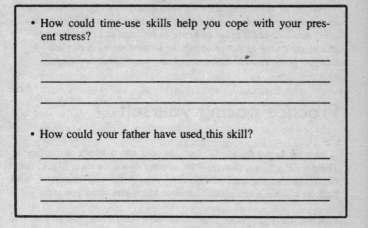

- How could time-use skills help you cope with your present stress?

  _____

  _____

  _____

- How could your father have used this skill?

  _____

  _____

  _____

Pacing

The art of regulating your tempo

When you tromp on the accelerator for jack-rabbit starts and jam on the brakes for screeching stops, you waste fuel and your car wears out faster.

When you work in sudden bursts of frantic activity, you waste energy and cause yourself distress.

Pacing is the skill of taking on no more, but no less, than you can handle and working at it steadily. It allows your mind and body to relax, because they know what to expect.

If you are surrounded by emergencies, feel the terrible pressure of time, or often run behind schedule, pacing skills can help you manage your stress.

Pacing in action

Instead of rushing around in a panic, Anne begins to pace herself. She figures out about how long each task will take her and stops trying to squeeze too much into her already busy days and nights.

Instead of staying up until the wee hours one night to catch up on ironing and feeling so beat she falls into bed at 8 o'clock the next, Anne makes a point of being in bed about 11 every night. She starts trying to eat at about the same time each day too, so that her body as well as her mind can know what to expect.

Practice pacing yourself

Try an experiment. Go outside and run a block at top speed. Then walk a block slowly. Run another block, walk a block, run a block, and so on until you're tired out. After you've rested, walk back at a slow, even pace. See how much less tired you get.

Schedule your time. Figure out how long each task is likely to take. Make allowances for emergencies that could force you to hurry. Then schedule your tasks to fill but not to overflow the time you have. If you have an hour, don't plan to do two hours of work.

Keep up. Don't allow yourself to get behind schedule. Just as important, don't allow yourself to get ahead. Practice plodding.

Be consistent. Try to eat your meals, sleep and exercise at about the same time every day. It will bring order into your chaotic life and will give your body a chance to prepare for the demands you're going to make on it.

STOP AND REFLECT

- How well do you pace yourself? Mark an X where you fall on the line.

Erratic	Sometimes irregular	Usually steady	Smooth

(Continued)

- How could sensible pacing help you adapt to some of the stressful situations you face?

  _____

  _____

  _____

- What proverb or adage applies to this skill?

  _____

  _____

  _____

10/ RELATIONSHIP SKILLS

Strategy #2: Change the scene

If you want to manage your stress by changing the way you relate to the people around you and to your environment, you can use the skills of:

- **Contact**—the art of forming friendships
- **Listening**—the art of tuning in to others
- **Assertiveness**—the art of saying no
- **Fight**—the art of standing your ground
- **Flight**—the art of retreat
- **Nest-building**—the art of turning your house into a home

Stress plagues Fred and Helen

"Fred, will you please just get out of my kitchen so I can finish making sandwiches? My garden club will be here in half an hour, and I haven't even changed my clothes!" Helen Williams exclaims in exasperation. *"Lately it seems you're always under foot,"* she shouts as he moves morosely out of her kingdom and into his—a small, sunny corner room nearly filled by a work table cluttered with scraps of silver, wire, jewelry fittings and polished stones.

Fred glowers at the work in progress. Lots of starts, no finishes. When he retired after 30 years as a jewelry repairman in a big downtown store, he'd had big dreams about working at home at his own pace, designing and crafting his own jewelry.

It's turned out to be more of a nightmare. Alone in his workshop, without the banter of the clerks at the front counters and the shop talk with the other repairmen, he can't seem to formulate or follow through on any designs. He feels cooped in and cut off. And when he can't work, he paces the kitchen. It's driving his wife crazy.

What can Fred and Helen do about their stress?

How might relationship skills help?

People may be the best and worst thing that ever happened to other people. They can be an incredible source of support for one another. They can also generate amazing stress.

Places are a similar source of great pleasure and sometimes even greater pain. Homes, offices, schools—any surroundings can be stressful.

Relationship skills help you reduce stress by changing the way you interact with those around you or by changing your surroundings.

Relationship skills are particularly helpful when:

- you aren't getting the support and friendship you want from others;
- you feel confused and need someone to listen to and care for you;
- you say "yes" to too many demands because you don't know how to say "no"; or
- your physical surroundings cause you tension.

Contact skills can help you meet new people.

Listening skills can help you form deeper, more rewarding relationships.

Assertiveness and **fight skills** help you keep the distance you need between you and others.

Flight skills can buy you time and space when you need to escape.

Nest-building skills help you create a physical environment that supports rather than stresses you.

Contact

The art of forming friendships

Switch on an unplugged lamp. Nothing happens. Plug the cord into an outlet and the lamp begins to glow.

Human beings need contact with other human beings the way a lamp needs electricity. Contact energizes people. It turns them on.

When people are out of contact with other people, they get tired, depressed, anxious. Contact can relieve stress, because it increases energy.

No one is born with contact skills. These are learned behaviors. Some people learn them younger than others. Some practice them more.

"I'm too shy" is just an excuse. Everyone is "too shy" until they polish their contact skills.

Contact in action

Fred sorely misses the contact he had in the big store downtown. He may need to bring a partner or an apprentice into his home workshop to share his ideas on jewelry-making and just to chat about politics or the weather.

He might sign up at the local recreation center to teach jewelry-making to adults one or two evenings a week and to youngsters on Saturdays.

Fred could join a shuffleboard or golf club, which he never had time for when he worked downtown. With this new outlet, he'd get fresh air and exercise, while making contact with others in his age group and neighborhood.

Practice contact yourself

Use conversation skills to expand contact. Remember, your best friend was once a stranger. Begin with an open-ended question. Rather than, "Are you a doctor?" ask, "What do you do?"

Follow up on "free information". Most people will tell you something about themselves. Ask more questions. Draw them out!

Offer some free information about yourself, to balance the exchange and to give the other person a chance to get interested in you. Talk about what you're feeling or thinking.

Admit your ignorance and ask for explanations. Everyone enjoys being a "consultant".

Trust the rhythm of the conversation. Each human interchange is unique. Some people won't interest you. You won't interest others. Don't worry about it.

Try new behaviors. Don't judge yourself by how well your experiments work. Just try a variety until you find ones that do enhance your contacts. Some possibilities:

Introduce yourself to at least one new person a day.

Invite someone you like but don't know well to have lunch with you.

Practice remembering people's names. Ask them to spell them if it helps you remember. Greet them by name.

Smile at someone in an elevator.

Hug five people daily for a week.

STOP AND REFLECT

• How good are you at making contact? Mark an X where you fall on the line.

Painfully shy	Shy, but I try	Sometimes I can	No problems

• How could you use contact skills to cope with a stressful situation you are facing?

_____

_____

_____

• How could you have used these skills on your first job?

_____

_____

_____

Listening

Tuning in to others' feelings

Empathy is a special kind of listening. It involves hearing not just words, but feelings.

That kind of listening doesn't come cheap. To hear and respond to the feelings of others, you have to turn your attention from yourself to them.

But you get something precious for the price you pay. You might get the stimulation of seeing the world from a different viewpoint, and you could get the trust, the warmth, the support and love of a deep, long-term relationship.

It's hard to get hurt if you don't get close. It's also well nigh impossible to develop the deep friendships you hunger for.

Listening skills can help alleviate stress by making the support system of such friendships available to you.

Listening in action

Fred recognizes that he's on Helen's nerves. She's never had him at home all day before.

He could take her out to her favorite restaurant, draw her out about her feelings and bite his tongue when he gets the urge to argue with her.

He can watch her face and posture, listen to the tone of her voice and try to stay out of her way when he "hears" a storm brewing.

Helen might try empathy, too, by asking Fred what's bothering him instead of judging him. When he tells her, she can repeat it in her own words, letting him know she really heard him.

Both Fred and Helen may feel closer when they listen lovingly and know the support of being heard.

How could assertiveness help you manage the stress you're feeling now?

_____

_____

_____

How could you use this skill to reduce stress in your church or club?

_____

_____

_____

...ght

...e art of standing your ground

...fair fight can clear the air and relieve a lot of stress. But you ...d to choose your fights—and weapons—carefully. Ask yourself ...e issue's worth fighting for. If the answer is yes, go for it.

...on't be afraid to fight with ones you love. Love and anger ...ally go together. If you didn't care about each other, you wouldn't ...er to fight.

...ust be sure of what you're fighting about. To get something ...structive from a fight, both sides must stick to their original ...oose.

...eople who never fight are likely to feel just as much stress as ...e who do. They swallow their anger and hide behind smiling ...ks. Maintaining a mask eats up a lot of life energy. And swal-...ed anger ferments inside and wreaks havoc on the body.

Practice listening yourself

Whose feelings are they? Make sure you distinguish between your feelings and the other person's. It's easy to get the two confused.

Accept, don't judge. What kind of feelings can you allow in yourself? In others? Learn to accept all feelings without judging them.

Read that body language. Listen with your eyes. Practice at a party. Watch someone across the room. See if you can tell what he or she is feeling. When you're talking with someone, pay attention to the feelings you see as well as the feelings you hear.

Paraphrase. Try to give people back a summary of what you just heard. That way they know you were listening; you know if you got it right; and sometimes hearing it from you helps clarify it for them.

Set up situations that encourage in-depth conversation. Try evenings in front of the fireplace with a bowl of popcorn or walks in the park. Don't be satisfied with shallow chatter. Pose deep, serious questions.

STOP AND REFLECT

• How well do you use listening skills? Mark an X where you fall on the line.

I try not to get involved	I can sometimes listen to feelings	I am very empathic

• How could you use this skill to cope with stress in your life right now?

_____

_____

(Continued)

• How does one of your favorite TV characters use it?

_____

_____

_____

Assertiveness

The art of saying no

What will happen if you say "no"? They won't like you. They'll be hurt. They'll argue with you. You'd feel guilty.

True? Probably not. But those fearful expectations force many people to say "yes" when they really want to say "no". And that causes resentment, which leads to a lot of stress.

If you often say "yes" when you mean "no", you may be neglecting your own needs, living to satisfy the demands of others. "We need you to be a room mother." "You must come to dinner Saturday." "Dad, drive me to Kirstin's house." There's no end to it.

Assertiveness skills will help you say "no" when "no" is what you mean, graciously, but firmly, and without excuses.

Assertiveness in action

Fred feels terribly henpecked by Helen. She drives him out of the kitchen. She interrupts him to send him to the supermarket for something she forgot. She laughs at him when he wears the Disney World T-shirt his grandchildren sent him from Florida.

He might say, "This is my kitchen too, and I like to sit in here while I'm thinking."

He could say, "I'm busy now. If you need it right away, you'd better go get it. If you can wait until after lunch, I'll go."

And he can say, "I worked 30 years to earn the right to wear

anything I please." Or he might even laugh along wi... agreeing, "It probably looks pretty silly." And keep rig... the T-shirt.

Practice assertiveness yoursel...

Respect yourself. You can't be assertive unless you... faith in your own self-worth is shaky, try repeating: "I... sible to and for me," or "I must answer for my de... "Others must wait for my answer and live with it."

Memorize assertive answers. You can use them,... but firmly, until they become second nature. Some eff... are, "No, I'd rather not; I wouldn't be comfortable wit... simply "No, thank you."

Don't make excuses. You don't owe anyone an explana... your answer. When you offer excuses, you open the... argument.

A limited "no" may be enough. You might want t... now but "yes" sometime in the future. If you really n... can say, "I'd really like to go out with you, but not... "I'd be willing to serve on that committee in the future... do it this spring."

STOP AND REFLECT

• How good are you at being assertive? Mark an... fall on the line.

I say what I mean	Sometimes I send mixed messages

Fight in action

Fred is angry with Helen for inviting her garden club over without warning him. It seems to him she's always having groups of women over, groups that exclude him, so that he has to hide like a fugitive in his own house.

He could make an appointment with Helen to fight about it. It would be dirty pool to start it now, just before her friends are due to arrive. But late this afternoon, well after they've left and she's had a chance to clean up, might be fine.

*When they do sit down to thrash it out, he can state his case without accusing her: "I'm starting to feel unwelcome in my own house." He'll have better luck if he avoids using "always" or "never", as tempting as it may be to shout: "You **always** have our house full of your friends," or "You **never** want me around."*

And he can let the fight end when the steam's run out, without demanding the last word.

Practice fight yourself

Choose your fights. Don't spend all your energy wrestling with every challenge you encounter.

Fight fair. Set an appointment for the fight and a specific amount of time to complete it.

State the subject clearly and stick to it. Avoid "always" and "never". Don't hit below the belt. On the other hand, don't wear your belt around your neck. If you're too touchy, too many topics become out of bounds. Don't drive your opponent into a corner. Trapped people fight dirty.

Answer back only after you've paraphrased what you've heard. And let the fight end when it's over. Don't demand the last word. If the issue isn't fully resolved, you can make plans to pick it up again later.

STOP AND REFLECT

- How often do you use fight skills? Mark an X where you fall on the line.

Never   **Occasionally**   **Often**   **Always**

- How could you use fight skills to help you cope with your present stress?

_____

_____

_____

- How could fight skills have helped you the last time you felt angry with a friend or family member?

_____

_____

_____

Flight

The art of retreat

Flight offers sure-fire, if temporary, relief from stress. It's a breathing space for the battle-weary.

There's nothing wrong with retreat. No one can remain locked in mortal combat without time-outs. Relentless battle damages the body, mind and spirit.

Flight takes many forms. You can retreat physically, just walk away from the problems that plague you. You can quit your job, leave home, drop out of school. Or you can make mini-escapes: home from a party, out to the mall, to your bedroom or backyard for five minutes of solitude, to the tennis court.

You can also retreat mentally, by daydreaming or fantasizing.

Feeling bored? Turn off what's happening and go somewhere else in your mind.

Flight is a coping skill that can easily be misused. Running away can become a pattern of avoiding responsibility. But used appropriately, occasionally, it's a good way to buy time to regain your strength.

Flight in action

Fred doesn't have to sit in his workroom and sulk while the garden club takes over his living room.

He can spruce up and head downtown for lunch with some of his old co-workers at the store.

He could go for a long walk.

He can go to a movie.

He might put his favorite lounge chair out in the backyard under his favorite tree, kick his shoes off, stretch out, close his eyes and go to Tahiti, or New York, or the north woods—or to the farm where he grew up or his first real romance.

Practice flight yourself

Escape physically. When stress builds up, disappear for 24 hours. Tell only one person where you're going.

Learn to fantasize. Try five-minute vacations. Take mental trips whenever you feel the need. You can plan, dream, lust, and no one will know the difference. Except you.

Divert yourself. Spend lunch breaks, evenings, weekends doing whatever helps you to escape. Read science fiction, go dancing, work jigsaw puzzles, refinish furniture. Anything that takes you away from yourself and your problems for a while.

Give it 24 hours. Sleep on every major decision. After you have struggled through a major life move and have settled on a course of action, wait 24 hours before setting it in motion. If it still feels right, jump in with confidence.

STOP AND REFLECT

• How often do you use flight skills? Mark an X where you fall on the line.

_____

Never   **Occasionally**   **Often**   **Always**

• How could you use flight techniques to adapt to stress you currently face?

_____

_____

_____

• How might you use this skill at a party?

_____

_____

_____

Nest-building

Turning your house into a home

All day you have to cope with a variety of environments that are beyond your control—an office, a hospital, a school, a church. You have to interact with different people. You have to drive through the traffic. You end up feeling stress.

You don't need a living environment that adds to that stress. You want a personal space that soothes and nurtures you.

You can create that kind of space. You can make it comfortable, quiet, inviting. You can fill it with things that are meaningful to you.

You can make your house a home with nest-building skills.

Nest-building in action

Fred is finding it hard to work at home and hard to relax around his wife's friends.

He can clean up the clutter on his work table. When he separates the silver from the gold, the clasps from the gemstones and cleans off a good, wide space near the window where he can work on his designs, Fred may find he's cleaned up his mind and allowed his creativity to start flowing as well.

He could move his favorite chair, the big leather recliner with the foot rest, into his work room. That way it is accessible to him even when the women are in the living room, and when he isn't working, he can lean back and plan, or daydream, or nap.

Fred might repaint the kitchen. He never liked it blue anyway. A sunny yellow would be more cheerful! And that would please Helen so much she might share the space with him more willingly.

Practice nest-building yourself

Throw out the clutter. Gather up unused furniture, clothes you haven't worn for months, piles of newspapers or magazines, extra cooking utensils, and throw them away, recycle them or give them to someone who could use them.

Decorate for comfort. Move your most comfortable chairs into the room where you spend the most time relaxing. Keep three of your favorite books right by your reading chair. Arrange lamps so you have good light for reading, soft light for relaxing. Make a collage of your favorite photographs of yourself, your family and friends, your trips. Hang it on your wall as a visual reminder of the people and places you love and the happy times you've had.

Experiment. Play with radically different living patterns, just to keep life interesting around your house. For example, live by candle-light for a week; wear no shoes in the house; walk around naked for an evening; eat in the bedroom, sleep in the kitchen, work in the living room.

STOP AND REFLECT

• How good are your nest-building skills? Mark an X on the line.

My nest adds to my stress	My nest is a neutral environment	My nest really takes care of me

• How could you build your nest to help relieve some of the stress in your life right now?

_____

_____

_____

• How do you think nest-building skills could help you after you retire?

_____

_____

_____

11/ OUTLOOK SKILLS

Strategy #3: Change Your Mind

If you want to manage your stress by changing your point of view, you can use the skills of:

Relabeling—the art of calling a spade a diamond in the rough
Surrender—the art of letting go
Faith—the art of accepting the mysterious and unknowable
Whispering—the art of giving yourself positive messages
Imagination—the art of creativity and laughter

Vicki and Phil escalate stress

"I don't want you hanging around this apartment unless you're willing to help," shouts Vicki. *"Fine,"* Phil snaps, *"if that's the way you want it, I won't be back!"* And he walks out.

An hour later, Vicki is still sitting slumped in her chair at the kitchen table. Her throat feels tight, and there's a big, dead weight in her stomach. She feels as if she's swallowed a brick. She's afraid he won't come back, and she's afraid he will.

Meanwhile, Phil guns the car out of the driveway and hurtles across town, tires screeching as he wheels around corners. He skids to a halt in front of a bar where some of his buddies like to grab a beer after work, a place Vicki detests.

An hour later, Phil slugs down his third double and lays his throbbing head on the cool marble of the bar. "Well, numbskull, you've really done it now. You can never go back," he mutters to himself.

How can Vicki and Phil cope with their stress?

How might outlook skills help?

Even if your life is stressful—and whose life isn't at times—you ultimately control the way your problems affect you.

Just as you often increase your stress by the way you view the events of your life, so also you can decrease your stress by changing your perceptions. Whether you put your stress to work for you or let it put you out of commission depends to a great extent on your mental attitude.

Outlook skills can help you manage your stress by giving you new ways of looking at your life experiences. They are especially helpful when:

- you feel depressed;
- you have adopted a negative outlook on life;
- you're experiencing grief over a loss; or
- your stress comes from self-imposed pressures.

Relabeling skills can help you interpret the meaning of events.
Surrender skills strengthen your ability to let go of past treasures.
Faith skills let you tap into a source of strength beyond yourself.
Whispering skills help you remember that you are a worthwhile person.
Imagination skills give you a broader perspective and the gift of laughter.

Relabeling

Calling spades diamonds

You label every experience you have. "Exciting" or "frightening", "satisfying" or "disappointing"—it's your choice.

The labels you choose determine the effect each experience will have on you. If you paste "crisis" labels over every experience, at the end of the day you'll have accumulated a pile of problems. On the other hand, if you use "challenge" labels, you'll end up with oodles of opportunities.

After you've labeled an experience, if you don't like the stress that results, you can always paste a new label over the old one. If you've called your life a can of worms, relabel it "nonvegetarian spaghetti".

You probably need to relabel if you see more problems than promises.

Relabeling in action

Instead of sitting slumped in her chair feeling miserable, Vicki can relabel her encounter with Phil.

"I've finally expressed my feelings and cleared the air," she might congratulate herself.

Or, "What a relief to have some quiet time alone again!"

Or even, "Making up is so much fun, it may be worth the fight."

In any case, she's turned her problem into a promise and relieved some of her stress.

Practice relabeling yourself

Choose a more positive label. List your stressors and write down the meaning you assign to each. Now cross out each meaning and substitute a more positive one. Try this exercise several times a day, especially when you feel anxious, worried or embarrassed.

Put your troubles into a broader perspective. Step outside yourself and the situation in which you feel trapped. Ask yourself, "Fifty years from now, or even 5 years from now, who will know or care?"

Use delays creatively. Instead of getting uptight and angry waiting for the doctor or dentist, a delayed train or service in a busy restaurant, do something to stimulate your own growth. Read, recite poetry (or write some), admire the beauty around you, think about a friend, reflect on your life.

Adopt the attitude of gratitude. Spend one whole day being thankful for everything that happens to you. If you like the results, keep it up.

Brainstorm relabeling with others. See how many creative new names your friends can find for the weeds in your yard, a stern look from your boss or rain clouds.

STOP AND REFLECT

- How often do you use relabeling? Put an X where you fall on the line.

_____

Never   **Occasionally**   **Often**   **Always**

- How could relabeling help you cope with your present stress?

_____

_____

_____

- Who do you know who uses this skill a lot?

_____

_____

_____

Surrender
The art of letting go

As you move through life, you lose things. Some are taken away; others you give up voluntarily.

If you are unwilling to let go of what you lose along life's way—parents, lovers, jobs, dreams, youth—you spend your energy struggling to hold on instead of using it in more constructive ways.

If you can't give up one goal to pursue another, if you're dead set on completing everything, you may be dead before you complete anything.

Surrender means accepting the present. It doesn't mean defeat. Surrender is a willingness to live within your limits, to make the best of what is instead of clutching at what used to be.

It could be called "the art of saying goodbye".

Surrender in Action

Phil can use surrender to pull himself back together.

"If it's over, it's over," he can admit. "That relationship was ready to end. We've been growing in entirely different directions."

Or he could decide to surrender his pride and go home. "I didn't mean it—I'm sorry. I'll try to be more help around here," is all it would take.

Practice surrender yourself

Focus on something you need to let go. Imagine you are holding it in your hand. Talk to it; tell it what you need to, then say "goodbye" and blow it away.

Don't worry about problems ahead of time. Wait until they occur; then deal with them. If you cross the bridge before you get there, you'll have to pay the toll twice.

Accept that life is unfinished. Nothing in life is ever fully finished. To be finished means to be dead. View your unfinished business as a sign that you are alive. Look at yourself in a mirror and say, "I accept the fact that I won't finish everything today." Practice leaving some undone work on your desk.

Tell a friend. Openly acknowledge your limitations to a friend. Sharing the experience will help you learn to surrender.

STOP AND REFLECT

- How often do you use surrender? Put an X where you fall on the line.

Never	Occasionally	Often	Always

- How could you surrender a situation that is currently causing you stress?

_____

_____

_____

- How did your parents use this skill?

_____

_____

_____

Faith

The art of accepting the unknowable

Faith is your primary resource for dealing with mysteries. Why was my child born retarded? What is death? Why do I experience so much pain? What is the purpose of life? These questions go beyond the familiar ground of fact and logic, into the hidden terrain of the unknown and the unknowable.

Faith isn't made up of platitudes. Don't confuse the two. Faith is what your heart tells you is true when your mind can't prove it. It is the final extension of your powers of perception.

Superficial faith isn't much of a resource. Deep faith can help you deal with the stress that comes from confronting the biggest, most painful questions of your existence.

Faith in action

Vicki can call upon her faith to help deal with the stress of the fight and Phil's abrupt, angry departure.

"I know my life has meaning and purpose, far greater meaning and purpose than I can see right now," she might pray. "Please give me the strength and clear vision to go on from here, with or without Phil."

Or Vicki can say, "I believe that our commitment to each other is stronger than this separation. We can find a way to work this out."

Or she could recall her resolution to say, "I forgive you," the next time they had a fight.

Practice faith yourself

Take time to be quiet. It doesn't matter if you call it prayer, meditation or thinking. When you learn to love the eloquence of silence, you can move beyond the limitations of your physical situation.

Use tragedy to develop depth. Don't run from painful realities. Every traumatic life experience brings with it an opportunity for you to develop new insights, a deeper vision of truth.

Ask your friends what they believe. Just listen for similarities and differences, and learn. Don't try to sell them on your beliefs.

Make a place for ritual and tradition in your life. Religious rituals, family traditions, personal practices, all help give you a sense of belonging, of personal history and mission.

STOP AND REFLECT

- How often do you use faith as a stress management skill? Put an X where you fall on the line.

Never	Occasionally	Often	Always

- How could you use your faith to help you cope with a present stress?

_____

_____

_____

- How do you think you might use this skill when moving to a new town?

_____

_____

_____

Whispering

Giving yourself positive messages

You talk to yourself all the time, even if you don't do it out loud. You tell yourself how you should behave, and you tell yourself how you feel about yourself. What you say reflects your beliefs, and as you know, your beliefs guide your perceptions, and your perceptions cause your stress.

If you tell yourself only bad things, you're going to end up feeling stress. You know the kind of bad messages: "No one likes me," "Other people can see through me," "I always fail in the long run,'' ''I have no right to be happy.'' Most of us are experts at whispering negative secrets in our own ears.

Try telling yourself positive things. ''I'm lovable,'' ''I'm pretty smart,'' ''I learn a lot from my mistakes,'' ''I'm okay just the way I am.'' You'll feel a lot better about yourself.

Whispering in action

Phil could whisper positive instead of negative messages to himself. Instead of, ''Well, numbskull, you've really done it,'' he might try, ''Good for you; you finally stood up to her,'' or, ''If we don't get back together, I can easily find someone else.''

Rather than chastise himself for blowing up, he could whisper, ''Good work! You kept your mouth shut and didn't do anything you'll regret.''

Practice whispering yourself

What are you telling yourself? List on an index card all the positive messages you would like to send to yourself. Carry the card with you. When you feel distressed, prompt yourself. Take out the card and read all the positive messages, adding to them when you can.

Check out your beliefs. Maybe you're setting yourself up for a fall. If you believe that everyone has to like you, then if 99 people do and one doesn't, you tell yourself, ''See I told you people don't like you!''

There are many other irrational beliefs that set similar traps, such as, ''A real man fights every time he is challenged'' or, ''I must never fail at anything'' or, ''I'm too shy to meet people easily.''

Watch others. See if you can tell what they whisper to themselves. Some people seem defeated before they start. Others succeed against great odds. What are they telling themselves about themselves?

STOP AND REFLECT

• How often do you use the skill of whispering? Put an X where you fall on the line.

Never	Occasionally	Often	Always

• How could positive whispering help you manage your present stress?

_____

_____

_____

• When would you like to see your partner use it?

_____

_____

_____

Imagination

The art of creativity and laughter

Laughter heals hurts. It releases tension. It gives you a new perspective. It lets you see yourself as separate from your problem.

Creativity and humor share a common root: the ability to see and appreciate the incongruities of life. They allow you to say with a smile, "It doesn't make sense. The parts don't fit. See how silly it is!"

You can play "ain't it awful" or "ain't it funny" with any situation. The latter will produce laughter, the most powerful stimulant available. People who take themselves and their situations too seriously have trouble laughing. Their barbed jokes, their antics, their efforts to be funny end up as depressing as they feel.

There are others—like Auntie Linnie. She can't tell a joke all the way through without forgetting something, like the punch line. But people can't stay around her long without rolling with laughter, because she's so skilled at seeing what other people miss—the little incongruities of her everyday life.

If you're bored or depressed, dragging along a heavy burden, try Auntie Linnie's remedy. It's powerful medicine.

Imagination in action

Vicki could try applying her imagination skills to her stress.

"Isn't that hilarious—Phil took off out of here with his suit coat on over blue jeans. He was so mad he didn't even notice which jacket he grabbed! And he left his wallet on the dresser. I can just see him now, trying to make up a story some bartender will believe. I bet he's up to his elbows in soapy water, working out his bar bill!"

Giggling in earnest by now, she goes over to the counter, picks up the carton of milk which Phil had left out, the object of her initial outburst. "What is it they always say? Don't cry over spilt milk?" she grins. Then she glances at the date on the carton, tastes a little and screws up her face. "I'll be darned. It was sour anyway!"

Practice imagination yourself

Don't try to be funny. Just enjoy life's inconsistencies. Pay attention to the details of events in your life. Then tell others about the incongruities and see what happens.

Change complaints into jokes. When you hear yourself complaining, force yourself to retell the tale in a way that makes it laughable.

Exercise your imagination. Practice painting colorful mental pictures and creating humorous situations in your mind.

For example, picture a man walking in a rainstorm. It's pouring. He is wearing a new, three piece suit and marching with dignity down the street, an umbrella over his head. But the umbrella has no cloth or plastic. It's just a skeleton of spokes. Give him a red tie that's bleeding all over his white shirt. Now give him short pants, white socks and cowboy boots. Have him meet someone. What do they say?

STOP AND REFLECT

- How often do you use imagination to help you cope with stress? Put an X where you fall on the line.

Never	Occasionally	Often	Always

- How could you use imagination to deal with a situation that is putting you under stress right now?

_____

_____

_____

- How would your senior prom have been different if you had used imagination skills?

_____

_____

_____

12/ PHYSICAL STAMINA SKILLS

Strategy #4: Build Up Your Strength

If you want to manage your stress by building up your stamina so you can withstand long-term pressure, you can use the skills of:

- **Exercise**—the art of fine tuning your body
- **Nourishment**—the art of eating for health
- **Gentleness**—the art of treating yourself kindly
- **Relaxation**—the art of cruising in neutral

Andy Northrup suffers job stress

"Your sales slipped again this month, Andy. You'd better get out there and hustle. There are younger men who would love to have your job, you know." The sales manager closed Andy's monthly report with a snap and turned away.

Andy Northrup heaved himself up out of the low chair and plodded toward the company lunchroom. Maybe a cup of coffee and a couple of doughnuts would fill that hollowness he felt inside.

"Hustle? I already am hustling! Lois is always on me about it," Andy thought. "Always complaining that I'm never home two days in a row. Always reminding me that the boys will be grown up before I know it. And she's right, I'm on the road all the time. The customers just aren't there anymore. Doesn't that idiot manager know there's a recession on!"

He gobbles his two doughnuts and hesitates briefly before going back for a third, recalling his doctor's warning words at his annual checkup last week. "You're overweight and out of shape, Andy. A man your age has to start thinking about heart attacks." Andy shrugs and reaches for the third doughnut. Sure, he'd gained 40 pounds since he finished high school. But you can't expect a man

*of 42 to look like a boy of 18. "Besides, I need the energy," he
tells himself.*

How can Andy cope with his stress?

How can physical stamina skills help me cope?

Sometimes you just can't make the stress you feel go away. You
may have to live with it over a period of time. If so, there is much
you can do to combat the effects of stress, to prevent it from
dragging you down and making you sick.

You wouldn't undertake a cross-country trip in a car with worn
tires, bad brakes, a frayed fan belt and a rusted radiator. You might
be able to putt around town in it for a while, but it would probably
let you down on a long haul.

It's just as foolish to try to handle long-term stress with your body
in less than its prime physical shape. Improving your physical
condition can help you resist disease and give you that extra energy
boost when you need it most.

Physical stamina skills are especially useful when:
- your stress is due to circumstances beyond your control;
- you choose to push yourself too hard;
- numerous life changes have hit you all at once; or
- you've changed your life style to minimize stress, but old
  stresses aren't completely gone.

Exercise skills increase your strength and stamina.
Nourishment skills give your body high quality building materials.
Gentleness skills help you minimize the wear and tear.
Relaxation skills help you unwind and let go of tension.

Exercise
The art of fine tuning your body

Jogging, swimming, playing tennis—everyone seems to be doing
it, or planning to do it, or making excuses about why they're not
doing it. Most people sense that exercise is important.

Why? It's true that exercise can tone up your muscles and keep you trim, and it can make you stronger. But most important, exercise helps your heart and lungs work better. As your heart, lungs and circulatory system improve, a number of good things happen. Nutrients and oxygen move more easily to all parts of your body. Wastes are removed more efficiently. Your enzyme system stays in better balance, so your muscles can relax more completely. You sleep better, and your endurance increases.

Paradoxical as it may sound, you'll have more energy after exercise than you did before. Like any piece of fine machinery, your body works better when it's used regularly.

Exercise in action

Andy Northrup may have to sit most of the day as he drives his car from town to town, but he could exercise and energize by parking the car several blocks from his first appointment and walking from there.

He can take a swim, just a few laps of the motel pool, before breakfast to wake himself up or to cool off at the end of the day—or both.

Andy might sign up for Saturday tennis lessons and invite his kids to join him. This would give him a chance to learn not only tennis but also what's going on with his fast-growing sons.

Practice exercise yourself

Are you willing to do it regularly? Answer honestly. If you're not willing to exercise for 20 minutes at least every other day, don't exercise at all. Irregular exertion can do more harm than good. Your body isn't prepared for it.

Start slowly and build up gradually. Don't push yourself too hard. Start with stretches and light exercise. Know and accept your limits. Increase your capacity over months, not days. If you feel tired rather than energized after exercising, you've probably done too much.

Give yourself a warm-up and a cool-down time. Spend five to ten minutes warming up before exercising and give yourself the same amount of time to relax afterwards.

Systematically stretch every muscle every day.

Exercise with friends. It's more fun and you'll keep each other at it when your will power weakens. Or use exercise as time alone to reflect and get perspective.

STOP AND REFLECT

• How often do you exercise to cope with your stress? Put an X where you fall on the line.

Never	Occasionally	Often	Always

• How could regular exercise help you manage a current stress?

_____

_____

_____

• How could you have used this skill last year?

_____

_____

_____

Nourishment
The art of eating for health

You are what you eat. It's not just a saying. Your body can only build with the materials it has. If you want it to be a solid structure, strong and resilient, you've got to furnish high quality building materials.

Eating properly isn't easy. Foods are full of unseen chemicals. Packaging is designed to fool you. The produce that looks the best may be the emptiest of nutrients. The convenience of fast food counters is offset by the empty calories and over-abundant fats that fill their styrofoam containers.

Good nutrition doesn't have to be complicated. Following a few common sense rules can help you change your eating habits dramatically.

Nourishment in action

Andy could substitute a couple of apples for that plate of doughnuts. They're sweet, they're tasty, and if he'll chew them carefully rather than wolfing them down, they're just as filling.

He can carry crunchy cereals or celery sticks with him in the car, for nibbling while he drives—a healthy substitute for the potato chips and cookies he always has on the seat beside him.

In the hamburger and pizza franchises where he usually grabs lunch on the run, Andy can head for the salad bar rather than the grill. Or he can stop at a sandwich shop and order "real" food— roast beef or turkey rather than bologna or summer sausage, swiss or cheddar rather than processed cheese spread. And have them put it on whole grain bread.

Practice nourishment yourself

Design your eating style for lifetime use. Avoid fad diets. If you want to lose weight, eat less and eat highly nutritious foods—then exercise, too.

Eat hearty in the morning, light at night. A good breakfast gives you the energy you need for your stressful day. At bedtime, your stomach shouldn't be loaded down with slow-digesting protein.

Try fasting or a partial fast. Eat only fresh vegetables and raw fruits and drink only water for three days. It will help clean out your system.

Eat natural foods. Raw is best for fruits and vegetables. Steamed is okay. Heat destroys nutrients and water dissolves them.

Read the labels. Know what's in the food you buy. The primary ingredient is listed first. So, if sugar is the first ingredient listed, you know there's more sugar than anything else in that box of cereal, can of fruit, etc.

Eat pure foods. Try to avoid additives and preservatives. Cut out sugar. Eat whole grain breads and cereals. Go easy on coffee and alcohol. Plain water is a terrific thirst quencher.

Have a junk food disposal party. Gather your family around you, and make sure you have a very large garbage bag.

STOP AND REFLECT

- How well do you use nourishment skills? Mark an X where you fall on this line.

Junk food junkie	Could do better	Pretty healthy	Health food fanatic

- How could you use nourishment skills to help you manage a currently stressful situation?

_____

_____

_____

- How could your mother have used nourishment skills?

_____

_____

_____

Gentleness

The art of treating yourself kindly

"No one else could be quite as rough on me as I am on myself."

True for you? If so, you may need to practice handling yourself with kid gloves. Even the hardest-driving hot-rodder has a poet hidden somewhere deep inside—a quiet, caring spirit that refreshes and restores. But as long as the hot-rodder is hurtling hellbent down her track, crashing into walls, pushing herself and her machine beyond their limits, ignoring signs of trouble, the soft voice of the poet will never be heard.

Gentleness skills help you slow down, shut up and get in balance with your own natural life rhythm.

Gentleness in action

Andy Northrup can learn to listen to what his body is telling him. He can take a nap before dinner instead of gulping a couple of aspirin and keeping at it. He can drink the tomato juice without the vodka if his stomach keeps getting upset after breakfast meetings. Or stop trying to mix work and eating.

Instead of mindlessly staring at the TV in his motel room, Andy could bring a cassette player with him and listen to his favorite music. He can make a point of seeking out a spot of beauty in every dull, drab town along his sales route.

Instead of snapping at his kids for giggling at the dinner table, Andy might talk Pig Latin right along with them.

Practice gentleness yourself

Listen to the voice of your body. When you treat yourself too roughly, your body will send you warnings: an aching back, a sour stomach, headaches, a stiff neck. When you get these messages, stop pushing yourself so hard.

Do something gentle for fun. Develop a hobby that helps you get in touch with your internal poet: art, music, writing, flower arranging, knitting, photography, gardening. A pastime that draws out the quiet beauty within you.

Play for fun. Learn to be childlike again. Be silly. Have fun. Let go of the competitive spirit and just play.

Pay attention to the trip. Life is a journey, not a destination. Your life won't be beautiful when you reach your goals if each day along the way isn't filled with beauty. Look for the lovely in your path right now. Go barefoot once in a while. Smell the flowers. Look up at the stars.

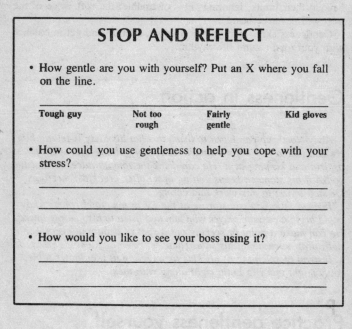

STOP AND REFLECT

- How gentle are you with yourself? Put an X where you fall on the line.

| Tough guy | Not too rough | Fairly gentle | Kid gloves |

- How could you use gentleness to help you cope with your stress?

  _____

  _____

- How would you like to see your boss using it?

  _____

  _____

Relaxation
The art of cruising in neutral

"I must relax. It's good for me," you say. So, with teeth gritted, hands clenched, jaw set and shoulders clamped around your neck, you order your body to RELAX!

It doesn't work. There are hundreds of ways to relax, to release tension. They all come from an interaction of body and mind, and they all involve letting go. Meditation, yoga, prayer, deep breathing, autogenics, guided imagery, stretching, progressive muscle relaxation, even yawning—are all ways to help the body let go of its tensions.

It doesn't matter which technique or combination of techniques you use. The important thing is to practice. You've had years of practice in tensing your muscles. You need to spend time and attention learning to let them go. If you don't, your body may reward you with cramped and knotted muscles, joint and back problems, fatigue, and eventually, limited mobility.

Relaxation in action

Andy can use progressive relaxation techniques each night before he goes to sleep. Instead of tossing and turning in a motel bed that is always too hard or too soft, he can lie quietly on his back and focus his attention on each part of his body, from head to toe, noticing where the tension is greatest, consciously tensing it even more, then consciously letting go.

In the morning Andy could try a series of limbering and stretching exercises, perhaps in time to his favorite music.

After each appointment, he can stretch and yawn. If he's afraid of attracting too much attention, he can duck into the men's room to do it. An empty elevator provides a perfect place for a relaxation break.

Practice relaxation yourself

Make a commitment. Choose any relaxation technique and practice it for 20 minutes a day, every day, for a month. At the month's end, evaluate your feeling of vitality.

Do a tension test. Check every part of your body, one part at a time. Notice which parts you are holding tight. Once you're aware of your favorite storage places for tension, you can let it go. Here's how. Consciously tighten the muscles even more. Then let it go. Repeat that three times. Imagine as you breathe in that you're inflating the tight muscle; as you breathe out, it deflates. Or meditate on relaxing the muscle until you can feel your pulse beat in it.

Take breathing breaks. Take three deep breaths any time you notice tension in your body. Give your body a break at least once an hour. If you're sitting, stand and stretch. Open your mouth and throat and breathe deeply, way down into your belly. Stretch and breathe until a yawn takes hold. A good yawn is like an orgasm— total tension triggering total release.

Get ready for bed. Don't take your troubles to bed with you. Do something relaxing just before bedtime—a long walk, a warm bath, a massage, a glass of milk. As you lie down, envision your body restoring and strengthening itself with sleep.

STOP AND REFLECT

- How good are you at relaxing? Put an X where you fall on the line.

I never relax	It's hard to let go	I relax sometimes	I'm very relaxed

- How could you use relaxation to help manage some stress you are feeling now?

  _____

  _____

- How could you use this skill when unexpected houseguests descend on you?

  _____

  _____

13/ ASSESSING YOUR COPING HABITS

An inventory of stress skills

What are my stress skills?

Now that you've explored some of your coping alternatives—getting organized, changing the scene, changing your mind and strengthening yourself—it's time to inventory your stress skills. What are your unique personal resources for dealing with the stressors in your life? Your options are by no means limited to the skills presented in the preceding four chapters, but these twenty can serve as useful reference points in assessing your coping proficiencies.

Start by identifying your present coping pattern. This will help you decide what old skills you'd like to polish and what new skills you'd like to master. Look back through the stress skills chapters. What strategies are you already using well? Brag a little! Affirm your expertise.

What underdeveloped strategies challenge you to grow? Be honest but not disparaging. What skills would you like to improve? What skills might be fun to try?

STOP AND REFLECT

• For each skill circle the number that corresponds to your typical skill use.

	never use	rarely use	use occasionally	use regularly
STRATEGY 1:				
PERSONAL MANAGEMENT SKILLS:				
Organizing yourself				
VALUING: Investing self appropriately	1	2	3	4
PLANNING: Moving toward goals	1	2	3	4
COMMITMENT: Saying "yes"	1	2	3	4
TIME USE: Setting priorities	1	2	3	4
PACING: Controlling the tempo	1	2	3	4
STRATEGY 2:				
RELATIONSHIP SKILLS:				
Changing the scene				
CONTACT: Reaching out	1	2	3	4
LISTENING: Tuning in to others	1	2	3	4
ASSERTIVENESS: Saying "no"	1	2	3	4
FIGHT: Standing your ground	1	2	3	4
FLIGHT: Leaving the scene	1	2	3	4
NEST-BUILDING: Creating a "home"	1	2	3	4

STRATEGY 3:
OUTLOOK SKILLS:
Changing your mind

RELABELING: Turning spade into diamond	1	2	3	4
SURRENDER: Saying "good-bye"	1	2	3	4
FAITH: Accepting your limits	1	2	3	4
IMAGINATION: Laughing, creativity	1	2	3	4
WHISPER: Talking nicely to self	1	2	3	4

STRATEGY 4:
PHYSICAL STAMINA:
Building your strength

EXERCISE: Fine-tuning your body	1	2	3	4
NOURISHMENT: Feeding your body	1	2	3	4
GENTLENESS: Wearing kid gloves	1	2	3	4
RELAXATION: Cruising in neutral	1	2	3	4

(Continued)

My current coping pattern

Look down the column of "1's". These are your underdeveloped skills.

• Underline the ones you would like to use more frequently.

Look at the column of "4's". These are probably your skills of habit.

• Mark those you tend to overuse.

• Which three individual coping skills do you use most frequently? For what kinds of stressors?

SKILL

_____

_____

_____

STRESSORS

_____

_____

_____

• As you identify your pattern of skill use, what insights and observations strike you?

_____

_____

_____

_____

_____

_____

_____

_____

STOP AND REFLECT

My future coping options
• Which three skills will most likely help you with your present stress?

SKILL

_____

_____

HOW IT WILL HELP

_____

_____

_____

• Which three skills would you like to develop further?

_____

_____

_____

• Which ones would most likely bring some laughter into your life?

_____

_____

_____

• Looking at the wide picture, what observations can you make about your potential coping resources?

_____

_____

_____

How do I master new skills?

If you want to expand your coping repertoire, here's the starting point. Pick one skill from your list and start practicing. Don't expect instant success. Any new behavior feels awkward at first—and often at second or third. Remember the first time you baked bread or drove a stick shift or changed a diaper or flossed your teeth or punched the cash register? At first you felt "all thumbs". Now that you've practiced these routines over and over, they're like second nature. That same progression from awkwardness to comfortable familiarity applies to developing new coping habits.

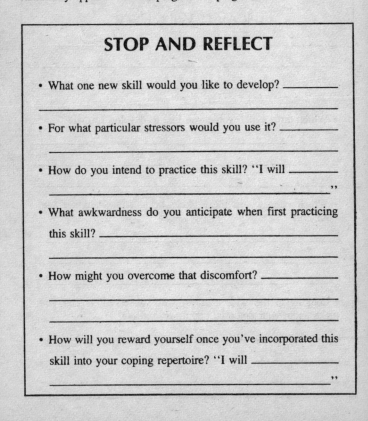

STOP AND REFLECT

- What one new skill would you like to develop? _____
  _____

- For what particular stressors would you use it? _____
  _____

- How do you intend to practice this skill? "I will _____
  _____ "

- What awkwardness do you anticipate when first practicing
  this skill? _____
  _____

- How might you overcome that discomfort? _____
  _____
  _____

- How will you reward yourself once you've incorporated this
  skill into your coping repertoire? "I will _____
  _____ "

Once you've isolated a target skill to develop, planned a strategy for practicing it and decided how to reward yourself, you're well on the way to establishing a new coping habit. Congratulations!

Before long that new skill will lose its awkwardness and become as much a part of your routine as brushing your teeth. You will have integrated that "exercise program" or that "up-beat attitude" or that "fantasy break" into your daily life.

Then it will be time for you to choose yet another skill and embark on a further adventure in coping.

THE END of
the BEGINNING

Picture yourself exactly 20 years from today. Stop for a minute and get the picture clear in your mind. What year is it? How old are you? Where are you? What are you doing? How are you feeling? How healthy are you? How peaceful? How relaxed? What have you done with your life? How would you describe its quality?

Close your eyes. Focus on every detail.

Do you see yourself fulfilled, at peace, the picture of energy and vitality? Are you still physically able to do what you want to do? Are you surrounded by people you love, people who love you? Have the years between now and then been satisfying ones? Full? Are your memories rich?

Or are you worn out, weakened by chronic disease, embittered over your unreached goals? Are you alone? Discarded? Depressed because life has passed you by?

Which picture is true for you? It's your choice. You're busy right now, working full time to make one of your pictures come true.

In the space below, draw a picture of yourself 20 years from now.

There's just no way around it—you are responsible for what becomes of you. You can't wait for your husband or kids or boss to change. You can't expect a doctor or psychologist or minister to do it for you. Only you can take action on your own behalf. Very little happens by chance. Most of it depends on how you choose to invest yourself now.

Is this the end of the book or the beginning? It could be the beginning:
* of creative change,
* of reasserting control over your life,
* of taking responsibility for yourself, your health, your life.

You decide whether this is the end or the beginning. You know. Only you can know.

Where do I start?

By now you may be feeling confused and overwhelmed by the variety of coping alternatives open to you. Which ones will work in your situation? Which do you want to try first?

An all-purpose coping strategy outlined in a book will fit about as well as a one-size-fits-all suit purchased at a discount store. Your coping plan must be custom-designed to fit you and your life—and you're the only qualified tailor.

The rest of this book is designed to help you tap into your own internal wisdom and to lead you step by step through the process of formulating a creative plan for coping with your stress. Answer the questions that seem relevant to you.

Be aware that planning is a process, not a product. There is no perfect plan and no plan works forever. Expect your plan to become outdated. Know that you'll need to revise it as you move on through life.

You'll probably want to walk through the process outlined here again and again, applying the questions to many different stressors in your life. Or you may want to come back to one or two parts that have been particularly helpful. In any case, approach the planning process with an experimental attitude. Be curious about your reactions. And have fun!

Step 1

Summarize your symptoms

First you need to recognize your symptoms of distress. What is happening in your life that signals your need to make some changes? Don't stop with the obvious symptoms like fatigue or headaches or too much smoking. Examine every aspect of your life:

- Your feelings—moods, joys and sorrows;
- Your mind—ideas, memory, sense of humor;
- Your relationships—family, friends, co-workers;
- Your body—strength, energy, pains, illness;
- Your spirit—hope, faith, sense of oneness with the world and;
- Your growth—future goals.

STOP AND REFLECT

- In all dimensions of your life, what symptoms concern you? What are your pains, your stuck areas, your dead spots?

_____

_____

_____

_____

_____

_____

_____

Step 2

Define the problem

Once you've identified the symptoms of distress you are experiencing, you're ready to figure out what is going on in your life to cause those symptoms. What is really at the root of your stress?

STOP AND REFLECT

Look back at your list of symptoms.
- What are some of the problems that you think might be causing those symptoms?

_____

_____

_____

_____

It's easy to get bogged down at this point and give up, saying, "See, my problems **are** overwhelming." Baloney! Everyone's problems are overwhelming, if they choose to look at them that way.

You can't work on all your problems at once. Don't try. For now, focus your energy wholeheartedly on one. Have faith—the others will still be there to tackle later. You may even find they're easier to manage after you've coped with the first one.

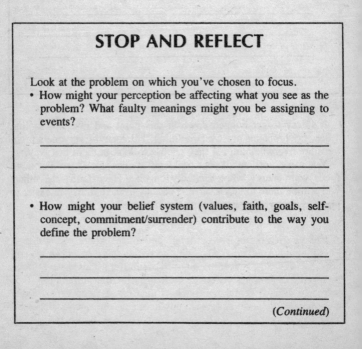

STOP AND REFLECT

Choose one of your problems to focus on for the rest of this planning process and define it as clearly as possible.
• What do you think is wrong? "My problem is _____

_____ "

Now that you've stated your problem, you need to restate it in a way that invites new insights and clear understanding.

Apply what you've learned earlier in the book to this problem. You may want to thumb through Chapters 1-7 to refresh your memory about what you've discovered.

STOP AND REFLECT

Look at the problem on which you've chosen to focus.
• How might your perception be affecting what you see as the problem? What faulty meanings might you be assigning to events?

_____

_____

_____

• How might your belief system (values, faith, goals, self-concept, commitment/surrender) contribute to the way you define the problem?

_____

_____

_____

(*Continued*)

- Is the pace of change in your life an underlying source of stress? What major changes have you gone through recently?

  _____
  _____
  _____

- How is your present life stage related to your problem?

  _____
  _____
  _____

- Could grief be at the heart of your problem? How?

  _____
  _____
  _____

- How is your problem influencing and being affected by your current life rhythm?

  _____
  _____
  _____

Redefine the problem

The way you define your problem determines where you will look for solutions. Stretching your mind to define the problem in several different ways can reveal alternative solutions that might never have occurred to you when you were limited by the first definition.

Poorly defined problems also lead to a lot of floundering. Once the problem is clearly and accurately defined, new solutions become obvious.

Suppose you are feeling anxious, restless, jittery and are not sleeping well. You might tell your doctor, "My nerves are shot. I need something to calm them down." Your definition of the problem has limited the treatment options to medication.

If you redefined the problem, you might open the door to many alternative solutions.

Instead of calling the problem "nerves", you could define it as:

- grief over my broken marriage;
- trying to do too much at once;
- financial worries;
- kids screaming at me; or
- too little exercise.

These new problem definitions invite coping options other than medication:

- deal with the grief, perhaps in counseling;
- set priorities and take one thing at a time;
- spend less, get a job that pays more, borrow;
- get a babysitter, whisper when you answer your kids, use earplugs; or
- walk to work, swim at noon, jog daily.

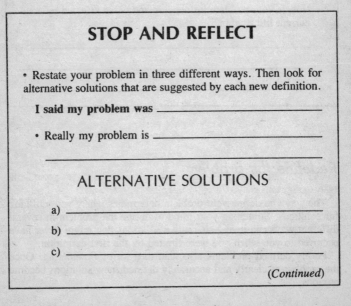

STOP AND REFLECT

- Restate your problem in three different ways. Then look for alternative solutions that are suggested by each new definition.

I said my problem was _____

- Really my problem is _____

_____

ALTERNATIVE SOLUTIONS

a) _____

b) _____

c) _____

(Continued)

• Or my problem may be _____

_____

ALTERNATIVE SOLUTIONS

a) _____

b) _____

c) _____

• Or perhaps it's _____

_____

ALTERNATIVE SOLUTIONS

a) _____

b) _____

c) _____

• Check the statement that most clearly describes for you the root cause of your stress.
• Mark the solutions that intrigue you most.

If you have trouble producing alternative definitions of your problem, ask a friend to help. Another person, who doesn't wear your blinders, sometimes finds it easier to see options.

If a coping strategy isn't working for you, come back to this step in the planning process later on and try redefining your problem. New definitions may suggest a novel approach.

Step 3

Identify your resources

Generals don't go into battle without knowing the resources at their disposal. Politicians don't go into campaigns without assessing their leverage and personal appeal. Before formulating a plan for working on the troublesome aspects of your life, you need to identify and assess your strengths.

STOP AND REFLECT

Make an inventory of your coping skills.
- What do you have going for you physically? (energy, strength, agility) _____

_____

_____

- What are your emotional strengths? (self-confidence, calm, empathy) _____

_____

_____

- What social support systems do you have? (family, friends, clubs) _____

_____

_____

- What are your intellectual resources? (creativity, humor, concentration, insight) _____

_____

_____

(Continued)

- What are your spiritual strengths? (prayer, social conscience, hope) _____

_____

_____

- How is your present life style a coping resource? (rituals, habits, hobbies, family traditions)_____

_____

_____

Refer back to your skills assessment in the previous chapter.

- What are your best stress skills? _____

_____

_____

Step 4

Recall what you've already tried

Undoubtedly you've tried several ways of coping with your problem. You may already have tried getting more rest, changing jobs, talking with friends, drinking, screaming or taking over-the-counter medicines. If they haven't worked or haven't worked well enough, and you're still feeling too much stress, don't keep trying variations on the same theme. Choose new strategies.

Cheer up! Let your failures teach you what won't work. Use your wealth of past experience to help you formulate a new plan with more potential for success. Don't give up.

STOP AND REFLECT

- What coping strategies have you already tried?
- Why haven't they worked?
- What did you learn from the failure?

TECHNIQUES
ALREADY TRIED

_____
_____
_____
_____

WHY FAILED

_____
_____
_____
_____

WHAT I LEARNED

_____
_____
_____
_____

- Ideas for future attempts?

_____
_____
_____

Step 5

Check your attitude

No matter how oppressive your problems or how aggressive your plan for coping with them, your attitude can either double or halve your chances for regaining inner peace. Why not give yourself every advantage? Cultivate a healthy and positive attitude.

You can take life seriously without struggling every step of the way. You can take yourself seriously without forfeiting your capacity to laugh at yourself.

An easy-going, confident, flexible attitude can help you let go of problems, stop worrying ahead of time, flow with the rhythm of life's ups and downs, relabel crises, cultivate optimism and focus your creative energies on solving the problem.

A positive attitude is itself an effective remedy for stress. It also makes your other coping plans work more effectively. So before you proceed, stop and check your attitude. Is it helping or hindering your progress?

STOP AND REFLECT

- On a scale of one to ten, your attitude regarding this problem is: (circle one)

1	2	3	4	5	6	7	8	9	10

terrible, hopeless	so-so, wait and see	positive, hopeful

- On a scale of one to ten, your willingness to work on this problem is: (circle one)

1	2	3	4	5	6	7	8	9	10

won't work on it	will give it some effort	will give it my best shot

- On a scale of one to ten, assess your sense of humor regarding your problem: (circle one)

1	2	3	4	5	6	7	8	9	10

there's nothing funny about it	it's pretty hard to laugh at it	I can see some humorous aspects

If your three attitude scores don't add up to at least 18, you might as well stop the planning process right here. You won't solve this problem right now. Your attitude is simply not committed, confident and flexible enough. You'd be setting yourself up for failure. Don't berate yourself. Just accept that that's the way you feel **right now**.

STOP AND REFLECT

- How do you feel about your attitude? _____
  _____
  _____

- In what ways would you like to change your attitude? _____
  _____
  _____
  _____

- How might you accomplish that change? _____
  _____
  _____
  _____

Step 6

Define your goals

What do you want to do about your problem? There's no sense constructing an elaborate plan if you really don't want to change. It's a waste of energy to design ways you could (or should) change when you have no intention of following through.

You may find you don't want to let some of your stress go. Accept that. Don't preach sermons to yourself about how you "should" change. If you don't want to, you won't.

If you've decided your problem is one you really do want to work on, the next crucial step is to define **clearly** the changes you want to make. Be as specific as possible. "I want to be happy," is a fine goal, but it's not very specific. What would make you happy? A good marriage? More success at work? World peace? A vacation? Not having headaches anymore? Each of these happy-makers suggests its own, concrete goal: improve communication in my marriage, apply for a higher level job, register as a conscientious objector, start saving for a trip next summer, get and use relaxation tapes.

Make sure your goals are clear. Your coping plan has a better chance for success if they are. If you don't know what you want, how can you plan ways to get it?

Also make sure your goals are consistent with your core values and beliefs. If the changes contemplated in your coping plan are contrary to your belief system, you'll probably sabotage any moves you make toward those goals.

You also need to ask yourself, "What do I stand to lose if I give up my stress?" The cost may be too great. Often people manage to avoid solving their problems because giving up the stress will also mean giving up something else that's important to them.

STOP AND REFLECT

- What would you like to see happen with your problem? What are your goals regarding your problem?

    General goal _____

      Specifically, I want . . . _____

      _____

    General goal _____

      Specifically, I want . . . _____

      _____

(Continued)

General goal _____

    Specifically, I want . . . _____

_____

General goal _____

    Specifically, I want . . . _____

_____

- Check it out. Are your "wants" in line with your belief system— your values, self-concept, long-range goals, commitments, etc?
      ☐ yes   ☐ no

- In order to reach your goals, what might you have to give up? _____

_____

_____

_____

- Which of these things are you willing to give up? _____

_____

_____

- Are there aspects of your problem you don't want to tamper with right now? Which parts? _____

_____

_____

- What moves are you willing to make toward reaching those goals? Be specific. _____

_____

_____

_____

Step 7

Formulate an action plan

The time has come. Time to apply all your insights in the creation of an action plan tailor-made for you.

As you design your plan, deciding exactly what alterations you want to make and how you intend to make them, keep these principles in mind:

Avoid impulsive, radical changes. Major changes add to your stress. Start with the smallest change possible. Don't try to repair everything at once. Be reasonable with yourself. If the smaller changes don't do the job, you can make bigger ones later. Beware of sweeping changes (moving, quitting your job, getting a divorce) as catch-all solutions.

As much as possible, choose coping behaviors that offer lasting rewards. Short-termers like running away or getting high can be disastrous on a long-term basis. Developing new friendships or embarking on a regular exercise program takes longer, but the positive results are more lasting.

Cultivate positive addictions. Instead of unhealthy "fixes" such as coffee, alcohol, drugs, aspirin, tobacco, valium and junk food, indulge regularly in activities like swimming, noon-time catnaps, playing a musical instrument, contact with other people.

Make the details of your plan very specific. Instead of saying, "I'm going to smoke less," say, "I'm going to cut down from 22 to 12 cigarettes a day." Rather than saying, "I'm going to be more friendly," say, "I'm going to invite Butch to have lunch with me this week."

Sign a contract with yourself. Make sure your promissory note includes a timetable. Specify what you are going to do, how often and when. Put it in writing. And read it regularly.

STOP AND REFLECT

- What change do you really want to make? _____
_____

- What **specifically** can you do to accomplish this change?

Strategy 1. I could _____

Strategy 2. I could _____

Strategy 3. I could _____

Strategy 4. I could _____

Strategy 5. I could _____

- Rate each of your possible action plans
  on the following scale.

	Strategy 1	Strategy 2	Strategy 3	Strategy 4	Strategy 5
Is it very specific?	_____	_____	_____	_____	_____
Does it avoid radical change?	_____	_____	_____	_____	_____
Does it have long-term value?	_____	_____	_____	_____	_____
Can it become a positive addiction?	_____	_____	_____	_____	_____

- Now, with these ratings in mind, what will you plan to do?
  Be very specific!

  I will (A) _____

  and (B) _____

  and (C) _____

Step 8

Spice it up

Now that you've identified your source of distress, pinpointed your goals for change and formulated a specific action plan, it's time to have a little fun. Add a creative, humorous twist. Ask yourself, "How could I make each of these activities more enjoyable?"

If your plan calls for an exercise program, it wouldn't have to be boring or competitive. You could run through the parking lot and touch every car, hop to work on one foot and home on the other, imagine you have infiltrated enemy territory and proceed to your office under hostile fire, take turns with your partner carrying each other around the house.

Or, if your plan calls for you to eat dinner out once a week, you might ask a new person to join you each time, dress in formal clothes and go to McDonald's, eat dessert first, go in disguise, go with a friend and feed each other, ask interesting looking people if you can sit with them, offer to wash your own dishes.

Don't just try to relax more. Try a sauna, take five deep breaths at every stoplight, yawn each time the phone rings, pay yourself a nickel a minute for taking naps.

You can double your energy and thereby double your chances for success by adding a creative twist to whatever you do.

STOP AND REFLECT

• Go back to the plan of action you just designed.

I plan to (A) _____

         (B) _____

         (C) _____

• Apply the list of creative alternatives below to your three

(Continued)

plans. How could you make each part of your plan more enjoyable?

make it bigger	do it alone	combine it with something
make it smaller	sell it	do it with friends
change its color	buy it	change the time of day
do it every hour	talk to it	do it backwards
do it at sunrise	simplify it	do it in a new place
learn from it	complicate it	do it with my boss
show my mother	charge it	ask a stranger to help
do it at midnight	laugh at it	do it with my clothes off

Instead of just (A) _____

I could _____

or _____

or _____

Instead of just (B) _____

I could _____

or _____

or _____

Instead of just (C) _____

I could _____

or _____

or _____

Don't stop now! There are scores of creative energizers. Brainstorm with your friends and neighbors. You could even ask a stranger!

Step 9

Act now

The rest is up to you. Only you can make your plan work. You need to commit yourself to a course of action and then follow through. This plan doesn't have to be your final solution. But nothing will happen until you actually begin to do something.

So DO IT!

Rx FOR STRESS

Summarize your plan and carry a copy of it with you, to remind yourself frequently of the goals you're trying to accomplish. If you can't write yourself this prescription, your plan still isn't clearly enough defined.

PRESCRIPTION FOR TAKING CHARGE OF MY STRESS

I, _____, am planning to _____
       (name)   (goal)

and I will attempt to accomplish this in my life by doing the

following: _____
                                        (actions)

_____

which will be done _____ and accomplished by
                          (frequency)

_____. When I've completed it, I'll reward
   (date)

myself by _____
                                  (rewards)

_____

    Signed _____

Step 10

Evaluate and revise

Once you've put your plan into action, keep track of changes in your feelings, your physical condition, your sense of yourself and the reactions of others. Get all the feedback you can.

Use that feedback to make mid-course corrections. Your progress may be slow or choppy. Some of your ideas will work well for you. Others may not work at all. Don't criticize yourself for strategies that fail. Your plan is never carved in granite. You can test ideas, revise them, test them again, until you finally hammer out an effective system for coping with your stress.

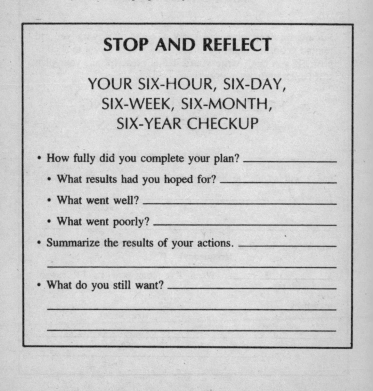

STOP AND REFLECT

YOUR SIX-HOUR, SIX-DAY, SIX-WEEK, SIX-MONTH, SIX-YEAR CHECKUP

- How fully did you complete your plan? _____
  - What results had you hoped for? _____
  - What went well? _____
  - What went poorly? _____
- Summarize the results of your actions. _____
  _____
- What do you still want? _____
  _____
  _____

Go back to Step 1 (Page 130) and use this leftover ''want'' as a focus for another trip through the planning process. Keep working through the process, fine tuning and making mid-course corrections until the plan fits you and your life.

Then get ready to move on and begin tackling the new sources of distress that have emerged in the meantime.

When stress returns, go through the entire planning process again. Don't try to start in the middle; the problem may be near the beginning. Be sure to keep written copies of your plans over the months and years so you can look back at them and celebrate your growth.

Bibliography

Books are like friends. Everyone selects their favorites. In this bibliography I'll introduce you to some of mine. Most are easy reading. They are listed non-alphabetically, ordered by my judgment of their relevance and quality.

General stress-related books

Selye, Hans. **The stress of life.** New York: McGraw-Hill, 1956. The classic work on stress written twenty years ahead of its time by the primary authority. Parts are highly technical but very worth reading.

Selye, Hans. **Stress without distress.** Philadelphia: Lippincott, 1974. A shorter, less technical book that discusses the difference between healthy stress and that which destroys. Includes Selye's discussion on life philosophy.

Pelletier, Kenneth. **Mind as healer, mind as slayer (a wholistic approach to preventing stress disorders).** New York: Dell, 1976. Applies current knowledge of stress to the medical practices of today and outlines implications for more effective methods which take this knowledge seriously.

McQuade, Walter, and Ann Aikman. **Stress: what it is, what it can do to your health, how to fight back.** New York: Bantam, 1975. A good general overview.

Levinson, Harry. **Executive stress.** New York: New American Library, 1975. A discussion of living with stress within professional and managerial positions.

Albrecht, Karl. **Stress and the manager: making it work for you.** Englewood Cliffs, NJ: Prentice-Hall, 1979. Clear, easy reading from cover to cover.

Goldberg, Philip. **Executive health.** New York: McGraw-Hill, 1977. Practical guide for managers and lay persons. Good compilation of research studies.

Davis, Martha, Elizabeth Robbins Eshelmand and Matthew McKay. **The relaxation and stress reduction workbook.** Richmond, CA: New Harbinger, 1980. Includes chapters on a complete smorgasbord of coping methodologies.

Adams, John D. **Understanding and managing stress.** San Diego, CA: University Associates, 1980. Parallel workbook, leader guide and readings for use in teaching.

Girdano, Daniel and George Everly. **Controlling stress and tension: a wholistic approach.** Englewood Cliffs, NJ: Prentice-Hall, 1979. Excellent resource from the wholistic perspective.

McCamy, John C., and James Presley. **Human life styling: keeping whole in the 20th century.** New York: Harper and Row, 1975. An excellent overall picture of the relationship between life style and health. Includes self-scoring tests for life style checkups.

Lewis, Howard R., and Martha E. Lewis. **Psychosomatics: how your emotions can damage your health.** New York: Pinnacle Books, 1975. A readable description of the way emotions can damage health.

Gordon, William J. J. **Synectics: the development of creative capacity.** New York: Collier Books, 1961. One of the original and still excellent books on creative problem solving.

Osborn, Alex. **Applied imagination: principles and procedures of creative problem solving.** New York: Charles Scribners, 1963. The methodology of creativity and problem solving from brainstorming through application.

Sheehy, Gail. **Passages: predictable crises of adult life.** New York: E. P. Dutton, 1974. The well-known and readable exposition of adult life stages.

Levinson, Daniel. **The seasons of a man's life.** New York: Knopf, 1978. The result of Dr. Levinson's years of research on adult life stages—a well researched work. Sheehy gathered much of her data from Levinson's work.

Personal management skills

Lakein, Alan. **How to get control of your time and your life.** New York: Signet, 1973. The best I've read on time use. Short, clear chapters with exercises. A must!

Bolles, Richard N. **The three boxes of life and how to get out of them: an introduction to life/work planning.** Berkeley, California: Ten Speed Press, 1978. A well illustrated, thorough system for analyzing your life goals and planning to achieve them. Focuses on the personal as well as the professional.

Scholz, Nelle Tumlin, Judith Sosebee Prince, and Gordon Porter Miller. **How to decide: a guide for women.** New York: College Entrance Exam Board, 1975. A workbook on making decisions and putting them into action. Focused on women—useful for all.

Winston, Stephanie. **Getting organized: the easy way to put your life in order.** New York: W. W. Norton, 1978. A helpful and practical guide. Sections on time, paperwork, money and the home.

Simon, Sidney B., Leland W. Howe, and Howard Kirschenbaum. **Values clarification: a handbook of practical strategies for teachers and students.** New York: Hart, 1972. The best basic book on values. Designed for teachers with 79 specific exercises for clarifying values.

Keleman, Stanley. **Living your dying.** New York: Random House, 1974. Poetic approach to interdependence of life style and death style.

Relationship skills

Jourard, Sidney. **The transparent self.** Princeton, New Jersey: Van Nos Reinhold, 1971. An important classic that claims people can only know who they are when they reveal themselves to others.

Miller, Sherod, Elam W. Nunnally, and Daniel B. Wackman. **Alive and aware: improving communication in relationships.** Minneapolis, Minnesota: Interpersonal Communication Programs, Inc., 1975. Communication techniques—specific skills for enriching relationships.

Alberti, Robert E., and Michael L. Emmons. **Stand up, speak out, talk back: the key to self-assertive behavior.** New York: Pocket Books, 1970. Still the classic—clear and simple.

Fensterheim, Herbert, and Jean Baer. **Don't say yes when you want to say no.** New York: David McKay, 1975. Assertiveness training—why for and how to.

Bach, George, and Peter Wyden. **The intimate enemy (how to fight fair in love and marriage).** New York: Avon, 1968. Teaches the rationale for and rules of fair and constructive fighting.

DeMille, Richard. **Put your mother on the ceiling (children's imagination games).** New York: Viking, 1973. Innovative exercises for developing imagination. Easy for children, more difficult for adults.

Zunin, Leonard, and Natalie Zunin. **Contact: the first four minutes.** New York: Ballantine, 1972. Focuses on the most crucial segment in any relationship—the beginning. Outlines guidelines and principles in detail.

Outlook skills

Mowrer, O. Hobart. **The new group therapy.** Princeton, New Jersey: D. Van Nostrand, 1964. The best book I've read on the relationship between psychology and theology. Discusses faith, guilt, and forgiveness in a "non-religious" but in-depth manner.

Colgrove, Melba, Harold Bloomfield, and Peter Williams. **How to survive the loss of a love.** New York: Bantam, 1977. Wonderful collection of prose/poetry and thoughts on the multidimensional experience of loss.

Westberg, Granger. **Good grief.** Philadelphia: Fortress Press, 1962. On the process of healthy grieving. Short enough to be read and appreciated by those in the midst of deep, raw grief.

Friedman, M., and R. H. Rosenman. **Type A behavior and your heart.** New York: Fawcett, 1976. Focuses ostensibly on heart disease, but is a clear guide to life style change for compulsive over-achievers.

Tournier, Paul. **The meaning of persons.** New York: Harper & Row, 1957. Classic on spiritual, humanistic respect for people—still relevant, thoughtful discussion.

Greenburg, Dan, and Marcia Jacobs. **How to make yourself miserable: a vital training manual.** New York: Random House, 1966. Hilarious instruction in self-defeating behavior, self-torture, and other goodies.

Thurber, James. **The Thurber carnival.** New York: Dell, 1962. My favorite joy taster. I take it out whenever my eyes need to smile again.

Physical stamina skills

Cooper, Kenneth. **The new aerobics.** New York: Bantam, 1970. A graduated plan of endurance exercises. Carefully explains the needs for taxing the circulatory and respiratory systems. The classic manual for building heart-lung fitness.

Lappe, Frances Moore. **Diet for a small planet.** New York: Ballantine, 1975. Unique plan for obtaining better protein quality by blending vegetarian foods.

Stuart, Richard, and Barbara Davis. **Slim chance in a fat world.**
Champaign, Illinois: Research Press, 1975. A plan for behavioral
control of obesity.

Fluegelman, Andrew. **New games book.** New York: Doubleday
Co., 1976. Fun ways to be—games focused on cooperation, not
competition.

Hendricks, C. G., and Russell Wills. **The centering book.** Englewood Cliffs, New Jersey: Prentice-Hall, 1975. Centering and
relaxation exercises designed for school but useful for all.

Bensen, Herbert. **The relaxation response.** New York: William
Morrow, 1975. A description of the physiology and technique of
relaxation.

Whole Person Associates provides consultation and continuing edu-
cation seminars in a wide variety of business and human service
settings. For further information on our services or publications,
please contact:

Whole Person Associates, Inc.
P.O. Box 3151
Duluth, MN 55803
(218) 728-4077